ZEALOUS

Zealous

Following Jesus with Guidance from St. Paul

MARK HART
AND
CHRISTOPHER CUDDY

SERVANT
BOOKS

PUBLISHED BY FRANCISCAN MEDIA
Cincinnati, Ohio

Cover and book design by Mark Sullivan
Cover image © Fotolia | MarFot

LIBRARY OF CONGRESS CATALOGING-IN-PUBLICATION DATA
Hart, Mark, 1973-
Zealous : following Jesus with guidance from St. Paul / Mark Hart and Christopher Cuddy.
pages cm
ISBN 978-1-61636-796-1 (alk. paper)
1. Christian life—Catholic authors. 2. Bible. Epistles of Paul—Criticism, interpretation, etc. I. Title.
BX2350.3.H366 2014
248.4—dc23
2014016005
ISBN 978-1-61636-796-1

Published by Servant Books, an imprint of Franciscan Media.
28 W. Liberty St.
Cincinnati, OH 45202
www.FranciscanMedia.org

Printed in the United States of America.
Printed on acid-free paper.
14 15 16 17 18 5 4 3 2 1

::: CONTENTS :::

It's impossible to imagine what the last two thousand years would have been if St. Paul had not lived at the far end of them. All the years since then have borne the mark of Christianity—the sign of the cross—and so much of what we understand about Christianity, especially about the cross, we have learned from the great Apostle to the Gentiles.

St. Paul was among the first Christians to set pen to paper to proclaim the Gospel. He looked upon the news of the day as it unfolded and interpreted it all in light of God's previous marvels. He took the great heritage of Israel and renewed its language for the New Covenant. St. Paul gave the Church the vocabulary it would, ever after, use to understand the life, death, and resurrection of Jesus.

We have St. Paul to thank for so much of what we call Christianity today. It's not that he was the founder of Christianity, as some people claim. But he did play a huge and unique role in the proclamation of the Gospel.

His name from birth was Saul, and he had been a Pharisee—an intensely devout and intelligent man, whose entire life was motivated by the expectation of Israel's Messiah. As a Pharisee, he worked to hasten the day of the Messiah's coming. He went so far as to enforce the strictest fidelity to the Law of Moses, believing that this would bring about the Day of the Lord. It was for this reason that he persecuted the Christians. He thought they were abandoning the God of their ancestors in order to worship Jesus.

As he traveled on his way, Saul met Jesus. (You'll read about this later in the book.) His encounter with Jesus was dramatic, but it wasn't a conversion, because it wasn't a turnaround, which is the literal meaning of *conversion*. It was more of an advance on the way. He recognized, then and there, that Israel's expectations had already been fulfilled, the work had been accomplished, the day had indeed been hastened, and the Messiah had come. It was Jesus.

There was no need for Saul to abandon the religion of the Old Covenant or radically redirect his zeal. Rather, he saw the signs and proclaimed the Day of the Lord, no longer in anticipation, but now in fulfillment.

Of course, this came at no small cost. It was a career-killer for him as a Pharisee. And then he had to endure afflictions and hardships beyond counting—calamities, beatings, floggings, stoning, imprisonment, shipwreck, hunger.

Soldiering on, he traveled the known world to announce a Church that was not just a reservation for the righteous, but was indeed universal, intended for Israel and the nations together.

At some point he began to use the name Paul. Still, his change was not a conversion. It was not a turning around but a bold charge forward, a rush, a drive. In fact, of all the apostles, it was Paul who most consistently kept the Church from receding back to the safety of a provincial reservation. It was Paul who kept the universal Catholic vision. It was Paul who proclaimed the power of the sacraments of the New Covenant. It was Paul who confronted the first pope, St. Peter, and urged him to live up to his own infallible papal teaching.

In the end, it was Paul who was impelled by grace, together with Peter, to consecrate the city of Rome with his own blood, shed in martyrdom.

Even today, after so many centuries, Paul's letters convey a personality that is overwhelming, a drive that is urgent. It's as if he cannot get the words out fast enough. We sense an excitement, but we can also be frustrated by his maddening compression of language. He rarely takes the time to spell things out, and he assumes that we already know a lot about the Bible and about the times that he and Jesus lived in. So we shouldn't feel too bad when we find St. Paul difficult. Even St. Peter confessed that, when he read St. Paul's letters, "There are some things in them hard to understand" (2 Peter 3:15).

St. Paul's energy, his richness, and his complexity can challenge us, and we shouldn't be surprised. We are talking, after all, about growth in "the grace and knowledge of our Lord and Savior Jesus Christ" (to steal a bit more of St. Peter's description of Paul's doctrine). Growth means development and change, and that's rarely easy for us. Sometimes it even causes us growing pains.

When we read St. Paul, we can sometimes feel as if we're being propelled forward by a hurricane, a tidal wave, or some other force of nature. But I've got news for you: It's even stronger than that, because it's a force of grace. Look at those maps of Paul's missionary journeys. Ponder those wide swaths that run the length and breadth of an empire. Imagine the momentum that made such progress possible.

And then remind yourself that the same momentum has not diminished. God's arm has not been shortened. When you read St. Paul, when you hear his words proclaimed in the liturgy, you're exposing yourself to the same force: "the grace and knowledge of our Lord and Savior Jesus Christ." And that can only be life-changing.

It can be fearsome, too, and daunting; and for that reason we can be thankful for books like this one, and guides like its authors, whom I count as friends.

Now, brace yourself!

Scott Hahn, PH.D.
Founder and President
St. Paul Center for Biblical Theology

St. Paul
The Spirit's Sword

Growing up Catholic, I looked at the Bible a lot. Note the verb in that previous sentence—I *looked* at the Bible a lot. It was the *picture Bible* we had in my house growing up, and the *pictures* got a lot of looks—the words? Not so much.

It sat on the third shelf of the bookcase in our family room. Rarely did it come down off that shelf for prayer as, again, we were Catholic and (unfortunately) weren't in the habit of reading the Bible with any regularity. It did come off the shelf for entertainment, however, because the pictures thoroughly intrigued me.

A PICTURE IS WORTH MORE THAN A THOUSAND WORDS
There was one picture in particular that always held my attention, even at only seven or eight years old, called *The Martyrdom of St. Paul*. A quick examination of our family Bible would have shown this to be the picture that got the most looks. The spine was so bent in that particular place that when one opened the hard cover, the book almost naturally flipped open right to this picture.

In it, St. Paul was kneeling as his Roman executioner wielded a sword in the air, just moments before Paul would lose his head.

He was being martyred as the final witness to a life spent serving God. The picture also depicted the presence of an angel, unseen by the Roman soldier but offering visible confirmation of God's presence during a moment of evil's suspected triumph.

The artwork was incredible: The colors were vibrant, the figures passionate.

And the truth of it was impossible to ignore. Truth takes hold of one's soul and subconsciousness in ways one might not realize in the moment but might reflect on for years to come. Little did I know that, to this day, when I would hear the word *martyrdom*, this picture would instinctively be the first image that rushed to my mind.

At the time, I had no concept of who St. Paul was or what he did. I certainly had no idea why he was being beheaded. I was just a normal little kid, and swords (and later, light sabers) caught my attention. The picture was engaging to my innocent eyes; it drew me in. Years later, I discovered the power of the words contained on the pages surrounding the pictures. Hopefully you have, too.

Martyrdom was the end of Paul's story...his *earthly* story, at least. But the martyrdom of St. Paul might not mean much to you if you haven't really followed the beginning and middle of his story. By following Paul's story, I don't mean reading or hearing it. I mean *experiencing it, walking it, discerning it,* and *praying it.*

Take a moment now, and ask the Holy Spirit to open your eyes and ears to something new as you read this book. Ask St. Paul to pray with you and for you, that you might gain new insights into Jesus Christ by focusing time and energy on the life and writings of this great saint.

Now, let's take a look at how this seemingly random man ended up martyred—how this obscure tent-maker from Tarsus could change the world in such a dramatic way that every corner of it would hear his words thousands of years later. Let's head back to the beginning of his story.

> Saul (was) still breathing threats and murder against the disciples of the Lord...as he journeyed and approached Damascus, and suddenly a light from heaven flashed about him. And he fell to the ground and heard a voice saying to him, "Saul, Saul, why do you persecute me?" And he said, "Who are you, Lord?" And he said, "I am Jesus, whom you are persecuting; but rise and enter the city, and you will be told what you are to do."
>
> The men who were traveling with him stood speechless, hearing the voice but seeing no one. Saul arose from the ground; and when his eyes were opened, he could see nothing; to they led him by the hand and brought him to Damascus. And for three days he was without sight, and neither ate nor drank. (Acts 9:1–9)

LITTLE DID HE KNOW

How cold and hard the earth must have felt as his body was thrust down upon it! The ground itself may have been the only thing colder or harder than Saul's heart that day. How brilliant the light must have been and how blinding the vision! That temporary blindness would later offer him *true vision* for the rest of his earthly days.

The road was little more than a path of dirt covered with small jagged rocks and pebbles. It was far from a desirable place to lay your head, much less land on. How humbling it must have been for Saul, powerful Saul, to quickly go from being the hunter to the *hunted*. How ironic that he landed upon the earth when God humbled him, for both *ground* and *humility* share the same root word in Latin (a language Saul certainly knew).

The dirt was caked upon his face. His vision blurred, but his hearing must have sharpened. Saul's companions stood speechless, but Christ did not.

In a flash, everything Saul knew, everything he had learned during his years of Rabbinical study, was rendered almost irrelevant. In one instant, he went from being certain of his righteousness and superiority among God's children to staring God in the face and going blind. The revelation was not only one of God's identity or Saul's shortsightedness; Saul's *self-righteousness* was revealed.

"Why are you persecuting me?" asked his new lord, *the* Lord, Jesus Christ.

How painful these words must have been to Saul. How many bloodstained memories must have rushed back to Saul's subconsciousness. No doubt in his blindness he recalled the faces of those he had hunted down and persecuted—faces like Stephen's. How gruesome the images, how deep the pain, and how humbling the guilt overflowing in his soul as he realized he had helped kill his own brothers and sisters, sons and daughters of his God and Father.

Those he had helped condemn, those he had called "apostates" he would now call brothers.

Can you relate to Saul at all? Answer the following questions, and record your answers in a journal for further reflection.

Do you look at your sins as not only greiving (or hurting) other people (your brothers and sisters), but actions that grieve Jesus himself? Think of an example.

How would you describe your experience or vision of God? Is it as intimate or personal as Saul's?

Do you feel like God calls you by name, and even *knows* your name?

Have you been feeling that God doesn't notice you or seem to care about what you do? If so, why?

Is your vision of God one of an absent Father who is far from active in your life, or is it one of a loving, ever-present Father?

If some of these questions strike a nerve in you (like they do in me), then perhaps your vision of God needs to change—just like Saul's did.

The God Saul encountered that day was different than the God he had come to know on his own. When Saul was humbled, he was startled; when he was blinded, he began to truly see. That's what grace does—it gives us the eyes of faith.

Saul was about to undergo the greatest change in his life. After encountering Christ face-to-face in such a profound way, everything about Saul would change—starting with his name.

When the Irresistible Force Encounters a Moveable Object

Many of us tend to think more highly of ourselves than we ought. Atheism is a perfect example of man, wounded and self-consumed, having a high opinion of himself. Atheists easily point to facts that show how God "cannot" be real, and they put far too much emphasis on their own logic and intelligence. In cases such as these, it's pride, not logic, that is the problem. There will always be a certain degree of faith necessary, but a hardened heart and a stubborn soul are too consumed with pride to embrace anything with the arms of faith.

Saul was a prideful man. Saul is like me...and Saul might be like you, too.

Even though we might picture ourselves as strong and immoveable, the truth is that when we encounter the Irresistible Force (the love) of God, something has to give—something has to change. God gives his love so freely that we are the ones who change: Love transforms everything. Confronted with the love, mercy, and power of God, we are reduced to rubble.

So there Saul sat, blinded and humbled. Everything he knew up until that trip to Damascus had changed, but it wasn't just Saul's world that was changing. God was doing something greater, something internal, something far less obvious and far more profound: God was changing Saul's very fiber and makeup. God was recreating Saul, to a certain extent; he was making Saul new, and Saul signified that by taking a new name. Saul became known as Paul.

Now called Paul, the future saint's understanding of his own vocation and purpose took on new meaning. He was already a man of strong character and courage, bold and passionate in defending the principles he saw as truth. His zeal had just been directed toward a prideful approach and violent end.

Scripture speaks of Saul dragging the early Christians out of their homes and condemning them to death (see Acts 8:3). While we can't condone his behavior, it's hard not to admire his passion, especially when so many people are so apathetic about their faith. As one modern philosopher explains, Paul may have been "moving in the wrong direction, but at least he's moving.

It's easier to move a car to the right if it's already moving...than if it's not moving at all."[1] Saul's desired destination didn't change; his route did. His conversion was not about changing his focus like most conversions; rather, it was about changing the means by which he pursued it.

Paul's calling and ultimate success (for the kingdom) should give all of us great hope. No matter how sinful we have been, no matter how prideful we could ever be, God is willing to use us, if we are willing to change. God has a plan for you (see Jeremiah 29:11), a plan he crafted before your conception (see Psalms 139:14–16), a plan that only you can fulfill (see Jeremiah 1:5–10).

Paul came to believe in this fact. And he didn't just believe in it, he preached it:

> For we are his workmanship, created in Christ Jesus for good works, which God prepared beforehand, that we should walk in them. (Ephesians 2:10)

We are created by God. We are recreated into Christ's image with the hope and expectation that we will do good works, works that God prepared for us beforehand. This is our vocation.

Often, we cannot clearly see or hear God's plans for us because we are so consumed with our own. God, in his love, finds ways to shake us out of our own best-laid plans (see Hebrews 12:26–29). The gentleness or force with which he shakes us normally corresponds to the degree of our stubbornness and sin. Too many of us, out of pride, run the other way; we choose the hard way. But, as Saul learned, you can't outrun God. Once shaken, we are broken, and only then can we be remade more perfectly into Christ's image. The formula goes something like this: shake, break, remake.

Paul didn't go straight from his experience on the road to Damascus to preaching; he spent years in prayer and discernment, growing in humility and preparation. It was later that he fulfilled his vocation as the world's greatest missionary. The question remains, though: What did Paul have that was so appealing for God to use in this way, for this mission? Was he just a guy with a lot of passion and drive? Just a man with a solid work ethic? He was a Rabbi who knew the law, sure, but he was also a tentmaker who was out for blood. What did God see in this religious fanatic?

To understand why Paul was the way he was, we have to understand Saul's background.

Need Change? Can Anyone Break a Pharisee?

It's impossible to understand what a radical change in perspective and lifestyle Paul went through if we don't understand a little bit about the life he lived before his encounter with Christ. Saul was a Pharisee, and we must understand this before we move forward.

If we were to take a survey of all the Catholics coming out of Mass on Sunday or, better yet, all of the Christians coming out of services on Sundays, the *majority* probably wouldn't know much about Pharisees. So if you don't either, rest easy—you're not alone. Pharisees (and Sadducees) are members of different Jewish sects that existed before, during and after the time of Jesus. Basically, a *sect* is a group of people with somewhat different or separate religious beliefs.

The word *Pharisee* comes from a Hebrew word that means "separate"; Pharisees separated themselves from most of society, which they considered sinful, in an effort to stay clean. At the time of Jesus, they were the popular religious political party (see John

7:48). They came onto the scene about two hundred years before Christ, when the Greeks were forcing the Jews to abandon their religious practices. What began as a good and necessary thing, however, became more of a bad thing over time.

What's vital to understand about the Pharisees is that they were very legalistic and followed the Law of Moses in extremely exacting ways (see Matthew 9:14; 23:15; Luke 18:12). They separated themselves not only from Gentiles (non-Jews), but from other Jews as well. While their intentions seemed pure, and their creed was solid, their religion was more about form and function than surrender or humility; they obeyed the letter of the law but ignored the spirit of it. They were very self-righteous (see Matthew 9, Luke 18).

As a result, Jesus had some strong words for them (see Matthew 12:9, 16:1–4). They supplemented the law with their own traditions, which took the laws an unnecessary step or two further than even God had designed. They knew the law like the back of their hands but not the front of their hearts. That's why there was such a rub with Jesus when he came onto the scene—they believed in the coming of the Messiah, but they denied that the Messiah was Jesus, even though He fulfilled all of the Messianic prophecies that existed in their Scriptures. If their hearts had been open, they would have recognized him. When Saul encountered the Messiah in Christ Jesus, Paul embraced the truth with unrelenting passion and urgency.

The Pharisees are not unlike many modern followers of God. Many of them are well-intentioned, highly intelligent, and very disciplined. They wouldn't miss Mass on a Sunday, but at the same time, they don't believe that the Eucharist is the true body and blood of Christ. They cling to rituals like the Mass, but they don't seek to understand the sacrifice behind the sacrament.

The Pharisees' worship, their religious practices, their speech, their dress, and their attitudes all reflected a very cold, impersonal relationship with God and their fellow man. They were still waiting for the Messiah, but they didn't recognize him in Jesus when he was right in their midst; he didn't fulfill their expectations. This is what Saul came from, but *everything* changed for Saul when he encountered Christ. Paul's interior change now forced radical change in his exterior life. His life was forever redirected and transformed from the moment he met Jesus.

Who Do You See in the Mirror—Saul or Paul?

Have you encountered God in a personal way? Do you know and relate to Jesus Christ in an intimate way? Are you more like Saul or Paul? Do you truly worship God? Do you go to Mass out of obedience or out of love?

If you haven't had that encounter in your life yet, that "aha moment" when you just *know* that God is real, Christ is present, and that you're a sinner and you need God's mercy, it's time to look again. What are you doing to give the Holy Spirit a shot at your heart? Are you reading the Scriptures and spending time in prayer? Are you falling on your knees and crying out to God to save you from your sinfulness, your brokenness, and yourself? It's never too late to fall into the arms of God. Prayer is not complicated, and it should never be scary. It's not about the words—it's about the posture of the heart. Stop and pray right now, and ask God to speak to you.

If you *have* had that encounter in your life, what have you done since then? Was it a retreat high where you said, "I'm yours,

Jesus," but didn't follow it with any tangible change? After you encountered God, did your environment change? Did your relationships change? Did your attitude, outlook, habits, dress, speech, conduct, focus, future, or goals change?

If not, ask yourself this question: "Am I letting God's will guide my life, or am I just looking for Jesus to put his rubber stamp on my own will?" If you've encountered Christ but have been reluctant to really jump in and change, now's the time. It's like a fire sale for the soul. Everything (you know) must go, so that God's will is all that's left.

In either case, a true encounter of Christ is like turning on the light in our souls. Sometimes it occurs on a retreat or at a camp. Sometimes it happens at a conference. Often during one of the sacraments, the lights just go on. Most of the time, though, it occurs during times of darkness and suffering. During those times, when we are most humbled and most in need, the light of Christ (see John 8:12) beckons to us in our darkness and, like a lighthouse in a storm, guides us safely to shore.

God's constant love requires a response on our part. If we are sincere, that response will be visible in our lives. St. Paul reminded his understudy, St. Timothy, of this fact when he wrote: "Set the believers an example in speech and conduct, in love, in faith, in purity" (1 Timothy 4:12). A Christian should be known by his love and his actions, not just by his words or titles.

Regardless of where we are right now, our goal should always be to recognize how we are like Saul—misguided, self-focused, judgmental—and strive to be more like Paul—humble, God-focused, merciful. This doesn't come easily; it doesn't happen quickly. But it doesn't take a literal knock-you-off-your-donkey encounter with Jesus to begin your own process of spiritual transformation, either. Christ is capable of giving us encounters just as profound as Saul's in moments of silent, prayerful meditation, selfless service, or true Christian fellowship.

Your own ongoing conversion and the deepening of your faith shouldn't be judged by the "how" of your encounter with Jesus, as in, "How is God choosing to speak to me?" but in the "what," as in, "What is Christ calling me to change this day, to leave behind this day, to sacrifice this day?"

The answer to that question requires being present to the God who is eternally present to us.

A New Portrait of Jesus Christ

You're going to find that St. Paul's writings are very unique. If you've never studied Paul's epistles before, you might think that they are a lot like the Gospels, recounting stories of Jesus and what he said. Actually, they are quite different.

Paul didn't write about what Jesus said or how he went around doing good works, healing the blind and the lepers, and so on. It would have been easy for Paul to talk about these things, given the time during which he lived and wrote, and the fact that Jesus's works were being passed on orally. There is every indication that Paul, too, knew the stories of the Gospels that had yet to be recorded in their full written form.

Why didn't St. Paul record the actions and words of Jesus like his apostolic counterparts, Matthew, Mark, Luke, and John? He wasn't an eyewitness of the events, but neither was Luke. St. Paul didn't have a historian's focus. St. Paul didn't just focus on what Jesus said and did, he focused on what Jesus's words and actions meant to everyday life.

Paul focused on Christ's *presence* in the present. Following his encounter with Jesus, he viewed Christ as ever-present, not as a historical figure. Paul understood something that many people back then and *still* today seem to forget: Jesus Christ is alive, and Jesus Christ is always present. Consider his words to those in Corinth:

> And he [Christ] died for all, that those who live might live no longer for themselves but for him…from now on, therefore, we regard no one from a human point of view; even though we once regarded Christ from a human point of view, we regard him thus no longer. Therefore, if any one is in Christ, he is a new creation; the old has passed away, behold, the new has come. (2 Corinthians 5:15–17)

St. Paul's understanding of Christ *present* dismantles the notion that, following his ascension, Christ went back to being God. Many people think of Jesus as a sort of human costume that God wore for about thirty years. This idea suggests that God sort of parachuted out of heaven into the manger, worked miracles, was crucified, rose, and then went back to heaven and took off the costume.

Nothing could be further from the truth. Jesus Christ is still Jesus Christ in heaven, only now in his glorified humanity. Jesus Christ is "the same yesterday, today and forever," as we are told by the writer of Hebrews (13:8).

St. Paul didn't want converts to the faith to view Jesus Christ merely as a piece of history. If you are living your faith strictly as a memorial to a dead person or a God who is no longer active, where is the motivation for a true relationship, one that is going to grow over time? St. Paul knew and proclaimed that not only is our Lord Jesus alive in heaven, but that he is alive in his mystical body of believers, the Church, and in his Word and the sacraments. After Christ made the truth of his presence *so clear* (Acts 9:4–5), Paul could never look at his fellow man the same way. He now saw Christ in everyone.

In Paul's writings, you won't get a list of Christ's accomplishments; instead, you'll find a deeper understanding of the personality of Jesus. Philosophically speaking, of course, our Lord had no human personality, it's the one human thing he hadn't got.[2] But make no mistake: Jesus is the human face of God. *God is Jesus.* When you see Jesus, you see the Father (see John 10:30 and 14:9).

What St. Paul does beautifully is to give us the person of Christ behind the works; he brings to light what it was about Jesus that was so endearing and so moving. St. Paul gives us a glimpse of why so many loved and followed Jesus, why fishermen left their nets, prostitutes stopped sinning, and tax collectors repaid those they cheated.

When you read St. Paul, you get a portrait of not just how to be like Christ, but of how to shed your own sinfulness and really become *one with Christ*—or a "little Christ," as C.S. Lewis put it in his seminal classic, *Mere Christianity.*

THE REASON FOR THIS BOOK

It would be impossible to tell you everything Paul taught in one book. Growing in spiritual depth and appreciation takes time. What you're going to read in the pages that follow is the broad stroke outline of St. Paul's theology. We're going to use St. Paul's most sophisticated written work, his Letter to the Romans as our blueprint. The reason for using Romans is twofold:

The book of Romans was one of the last works that St. Paul wrote, and in it we can clearly see how the culmination of years of prayer, preaching, and teaching came about. The result is one of the greatest books of the Bible and the greatest (non-Gospel) treatise on Christianity the world has ever known. It sums up the thoughts, goals, and thrusts of all of St. Paul's earlier letters to the groups in places like Corinth, Galatia, and Colossae. Put simply, if you get Romans, you're going to understand 1 Corinthians, Galatians, Colossians, and a whole lot more.

Romans is the book that has driven the greatest wedge between Catholics and non-Catholic Christians in the past five hundred years or so. Actually, it's not the book itself that has caused the wedge; the differing interpretations of the book created the rift. If all believers understood a few key words and concepts, Christians of different denominations could quickly see that our beliefs, though differing on certain doctrinal and practical issues, are more alike than we might think regarding faith and salvation.

In this book, our goal is to give you a basic understanding of St. Paul's core teachings (and enough tools to unpack those teachings) in the hope that all of his writings will come to life for you. The better you understand the man behind the letters—the one whose pen the Holy Spirit took captive—the better you'll understand not only half of the New Testament (which he wrote), but also the Gospels, the Mass, and the sacraments, as well as your faith, vocation, and role in God's plan of salvation.

See this book as our gift to you, not because we wrote it but because God somehow got it into your hands. God, the Living Word, wants to speak to you through his word in a new way now. You'll soon see why the Scriptures are "sharper than any two-edged sword" (Hebrews 4:10), because they'll pierce your heart en route to your soul. Our hope is that you will desire to follow Jesus Christ as zealously as St. Paul himself!

CHAPTER ONE

The One Beyond Question
Who Is God?

One of the first prayers I learned is a simple mealtime grace. It is memorable because of its simplicity and remembered because of the way it flows and rhymes:

> God is great,
> God is good,
> and we thank Him for this food.

Although short enough for a child to remember and recite, there is a lot of substance to this prayer. It expresses three extremely important points about God:

1. God *is*. He exists. He's not a figment of our imagination; he's real.
2. God is *great*. He is all-powerful and has ultimate authority over everything that he has created.
3. God is *good*. He is a just, righteous, and loving God.

All of this may seem simple and straightforward, but we could spend the rest of our lives studying, praying, and meditating upon

God's existence, greatness, and goodness (and some guys have!). Don't let it fool you: This is deep stuff.

Life is interesting. Most of us learn about the Lord at an early age. It is usually our parents, grandparents or friends who first tell us about this powerful being called "God." Sometimes, he's used as a threat: "If you do bad things, God will be angry and he'll punish you." Other times, he's used as an incentive: "God will reward you if you're good." And still, other times, he is something thrown about as a common curse word.

But this raises the question: *Who,* exactly, is God? Or even, *What* is God? Is he a cosmic force somewhere up in the sky? An invisible man watching our every move, recording every good (and bad) thing we do? Is he a celestial Santa Claus or a heavenly genie that has an unending supply of gifts to give and wishes to grant?

Is he powerful enough to do whatever he wants? Is he considerate enough to help us with the things *we* want? Does he care about us? Is he personal? Is he kind? These are all very important questions that everyone asks at least once in their lives. St. Paul's letter to the Romans has the answers to these and other significant issues.

Are You For Real?

If you were to walk down a street in your hometown and perform a random poll, asking, "Do you believe God exists?", most people would say that they do. Atheists—those who deny the existence of God—aren't all that common, although their numbers are growing in our increasingly secular culture. Sometimes people just have a very small view of God. Other times, they believe that he's somewhere out in space, totally disconnected from our life and world. Many people are agnostic—not totally denying that there is a supreme being somewhere doing something, but not really having any personal sense of him either. You may not like God. You may not care about him. You may erroneously think that he doesn't care about you. But we're going to suggest that it is reasonable to believe that he exists. Again, whether you think he's a power, a spirit, an entity, or a force, there are compelling reasons to believe that he *is*, and this book is written with that assumption in mind.

Isn't it remarkable that so many people believe that God exists? How do we know that he's real? Most of us have not heard him speak audibly. We can't see him looking down at us from heaven. We've never passed him on the street. There are no divine billboards saying things like, "God is real!" And yet somehow we all have a sense that God exists. How can this be?

Good questions! Indeed, how do we know that God exists? We don't believe in the tooth fairy. No one has ever seen the Easter Bunny. Most of us eventually discovered that Santa's elves were really our parents. But not so with God. People of all ages—old and young—believe in the existence of God. People from all countries and nationalities worship him. Yet none of us has ever laid eyes upon him, touched him, smelled him, or heard his voice. How do we know that he's real?

The apostle Paul faced similar questions almost two thousand years ago, and his answers are still relevant to us today. St. Paul taught that even though we don't hear an audible voice from heaven or pass him on the sidewalk, everyone knows that God is real because he has clearly revealed himself to us. "For what can be known about God is plain," St. Paul says; and the reason for this is simple: "Because God has shown it" to us all (Romans 1:19).

The existence of God is not a secret. The question of his reality is not an unsolved mystery. God's presence is not something we have to decode—he made it easy for us. *God has revealed himself to us. He has shown us that he exists.*

But this raises another question: "How has God revealed himself?" We don't hear his voice from heaven shouting, "Hey, I'm up here!" We don't receive heavenly e-mails or text messages from a divine cell phone. He hasn't faxed us a picture of himself. So *how* has he revealed himself?

Being the divinely inspired genius that he was, St. Paul anticipated this question and gave a powerful answer.

> Ever since the creation of the world his invisible nature, namely, his eternal power and deity, has been clearly perceived in the things that have been made. (Romans 1:20)

How has God revealed himself to us? *He has revealed himself to us in and through the things he has made.* We see traces of God in the created world around us.

WHODUNIT?

Detective shows are very popular. It is fascinating to learn how investigators gather clues and evidence in order to figure out whodunit—who committed the crime. One of the most common and useful tools law enforcement officials use to catch culprits is the *fingerprint.* If cops discover someone's fingerprints on the murder weapon, chances are pretty good that the person was, at least partially, involved with the crime. The fingerprints show that the person had contact with the scene of the crime. One of the things television shows like *CSI* and *Law and Order* tell us is this: *We always leave behind traces of our presence everywhere we go.*

No matter how careful someone is, there will always be a finger-print, a strand of hair, or a clothing fiber left behind that reveals something about the person who was there.

The same is true with God and the world. When God created the universe, he left behind "fingerprints" of sorts. There are traces of his presence in the world; this is nothing new or revolutionary. The Bible has said this all along. The book of Wisdom tells us that all created things reveal the existence of their craftsman (see Wisdom 13:1). Furthermore, St. Paul taught that God designed all things in such a way that people would know that he exists and would seek after him (see Acts 17:26). The *Catechism of the Catholic Church* states this as well:

> God speaks to man through the visible creation. The material cosmos is presented to man's intelligence that he can read the traces of its Creator. Light and darkness, wind and fire, water and earth, the tree and its fruits speak of God and symbolize both his greatness and his nearness. (CCC 1147)

This is not a revolutionary concept. It is really just plain old common sense. If I hear a knock on the door, I know that someone or something has to be the knocker. If I receive a phone call, there has to be a caller. Whenever something happens, it happens because something caused it to happen. Things don't just happen by themselves.

The very fact that there is such a thing as creation (the universe in which we live) points to the fact that there must be a creator. Something cannot come from nothing. And the fact that there is something at all—and, in our case, many different things in this vast world—tells us that there has to be something that made it. (For more on this, see CCC 31–34.)

Do We Really Get it?

Our knowledge of God's existence is not a possible or hypothetical knowledge. St. Paul emphasizes the fact that God's existence is plain because "God has shown" his existence to all of us (see Romans 1:19). The *Catechism* tells us that we can be *certain* about the existence of God by observing his work in creation (see CCC 31). God has shown himself to us, and his nature has been "clearly perceived in the things that have been made" (Romans 1:20).

In reality, everyone gets it. In fact, everyone sees God's existence so clearly that they "have no excuse" (Romans 2:1). No one will ever be able to stand before the judgment seat of God and say, "I didn't know you were real because you didn't give me enough clues."

But this raises another question: "If God's existence is so obvious and clear, why do some people still seem to miss it?"

Another good question. There does seem to be a problem with all of this. God exists. The Bible says we know this because he has clearly revealed himself to us. But the fact remains: Some people still don't believe that God exists. A few authors have recently written very popular books arguing that people are foolish if they believe in the existence of God. This is troubling. If God has really so clearly revealed himself, how is it that people don't always see it?

If there really is a God, then why are there atheists?

St. Paul has some very strong words to say about this issue. He doesn't beat around the bush. The apostle tells it like it is. He says that there have been people who "knew God [but] did not honor him as God," and as a result "they became futile in their thinking and their senseless minds were darkened." This is tragic because although they were "claiming to be wise," they "became fools" in their denial of God's existence. St. Paul shoots straight with us and gives us an answer that is razor-sharp in accuracy and precision—so sharp that it's hard for us to accept at times:

> For although they knew God they did not honor him as God or give thanks to him, but they became futile in their thinking and their senseless minds were darkened. Claiming to be wise, they became fools, and exchanged the glory of the immortal God for images resembling mortal man or birds or animals or reptiles. (Romans 1:21–23)

The apostle couldn't be any clearer: people *do* know that there is a God. His existence is "clearly perceived" (Romans 1:20), but sin has caused many of us to become "futile" in our thinking and the light of truth in our minds has been "darkened" to such a degree that we have lost all sense of that which is obvious (Romans 1:21). The truth is so clear, but sin clouds the mind and blinds us to that which is evident.

Atheism isn't so much a problem of the mind as it is a problem of the *heart*. There aren't atheists because God hasn't clearly revealed himself; there are atheists because of sin and its effects. Atheism is a spiritual problem, not an intellectual problem. St. Paul taught that the only way for you *not* to recognize God's existence is if you don't *want* to recognize his existence. If someone denies the existence of God, the problem is found in the person, not in God.

How can this be? Why would anyone be so antagonistic to the concept of God?

The answer is simple: We exchange higher things for lower things. We would rather follow and worship anything but the one true God who created everything. Although most of us wouldn't worship something as ridiculous as a bird or reptile, our idolatry is just as awful and ten times more sophisticated.

We may not worship our pet parakeet, but we let ourselves get sucked into the clutches of pop culture. Our idols are no longer plants and animals. No, today we worship things like social media, movies, sports, food, and entertainment. These are the idols that presently enslave our culture. And what makes matters worse is the fact that *many of us don't even realize that we're worshipping false gods.* We're so in love with the latest electronic gizmos, sports teams, and media gossip that we don't even stop to notice—much less adore—the creator of the universe.

A recent study done by the Bureau of Labor Statistics states that the average American spends less than three minutes a day on "religious and spiritual activities."[3] Spiritual activities, like prayer, were ranked the most infrequent of all activities. We are so consumed with the things of the created world that we forget that there even is a creator! This is the essence of idolatry. We gladly follow anything other than a God who makes demands on us and tell us what to do with our money, our bodies, our time... our lives.

We will examine the nature of sin and its deadly effects more in the next chapter, but suffice it to say that St. Paul warns us to avoid this pitiful insanity. Someone is insane when he or she doesn't see things as they really are. If I were to run down the street screaming, "The unicorns are trying to eat me!" I would be considered crazy. Why? For a very simple reason: Unicorns do not exist. There is no such thing as a horse with a horn coming out of its head. They are not a part of reality. I would be a fool if I spent my whole life in a fantasy world that doesn't really exist, thinking that the imaginary is real and that the real is imaginary.

St. Paul eagerly desired that we not let our view of reality become so distorted that we think that the truth is a lie and a lie is the truth. Those "claiming to be wise" really become "fools" who exchange "the glory of the immortal God for images resembling mortal man or birds or animals or reptiles" (Romans 1:22–23)— or movies, sex, the Internet, or anything else. The apostle wants to save us from spiritual insanity.

A wasted life is a life lived without worshiping God. A life well-lived is a life spent in his presence and offered for his glory (see 1 Corinthians 10:31).

God Is Great

So far we've seen that God is real, that he exists, that he's not just a figment of our imagination. And now we come to another equally important question: *What* or *who* is God? It's one thing to recognize *that* he exists. It's quite another thing to discover what he's *like*. What kind of personality does he have? Does he care about what's going on down here?

As the mealtime grace tells us: God is great. He is powerful.

The greatness and power of God is essential to our faith. At every Sunday Mass we recite the following words: "I believe in one God, the Father almighty, maker of heaven and earth…" It is fascinating that of all the things the Creed could say about God it focuses on his power: "God, the Father *almighty*." God is no wimp. He is omnipotent. That means he is all-powerful. The *Catechism* states:

Of all the divine attributes, only God's omnipotence is named in the Creed: to confess this power has great bearing on our lives. We believe that His might is *universal*, for God who created everything also rules everything and can do everything. (CCC 268; emphasis in original)

God's might and power have no external limits. There is nothing greater, stronger, or bigger than God. He is almighty overall, and over *all*.

The Sovereign Author

In order to help us understand just how great God really is, the Church teaches that God is sovereign. *Sovereignty* is not a word that is commonly understood in our American culture. This is a shame because it is one of the most profound and comforting things about God. Sovereignty, in its most basic meaning, refers to authority. When we speak of the sovereignty of God, we are referring to his ultimate and supreme authority over everything.

Now, authority is something we are all too familiar with, and many of us shy away from it. The very word *authority* conjures up images of parents, teachers, and police—all who inflict their stifling rules and regulations upon us. Most of us would prefer to be left alone so we can do our own thing. The less authority people exercise over us the better.

The sovereign authority of God is different from human authority, however. His authority is never unjust or oppressive. In fact, the sovereignty of God is one of the most comforting and powerful expressions of his *love*.

The word *authority* is fitting for God because even in the word itself we can see the word *author*. God is the author of all things—he created everything that exists—and thus he has ultimate *authority* over all things. He is in control. He is fully aware of all that has happened, that is happening, and that will happen. He has a plan for your life, for the world, for everything. The *Catechism* speaks of God being the "sovereign master of his plan" (CCC 306). From God's perspective, there are no accidents. There is no such thing as luck or chance.

Albert Einstein is famous for saying "God doesn't play dice."[4] God knows all that will happen. He is never surprised by the events that occur. He is in control of everything. He even knows how many hairs are on your head (see Luke 12:7). God knew you perfectly even before you were even created (see Jeremiah 1:5).

There are no limits to God's power, God's greatness, or God's knowledge. St. Paul speaks of the "immeasurable greatness of his power" (Ephesians 1:19). In fact, he is the source of true power (2 Corinthians 4:7). If I want to get stronger, I have to go to the gym, lift weights, and work out. If I want to increase my strength, I must work for it. This is not the case with God. He didn't have to earn his power and authority. His power is eternal. It has no beginning or end (see Romans 1:20). And St. Paul tells us that our faith does "not rest in the wisdom of men but in the power of God" (1 Corinthians 2:5).

This is a critical point. It is easy for us to become smug in our own power, talents, and abilities. This is dangerous—our power is very limited, and we are finite creatures. God is infinite. We were created. He is eternal. In fact, God is so great that St. Paul notes that "the foolishness of God is wiser than men, and the weakness of God is stronger than man" (1 Corinthians 1:25). God is the creator, the author of everything. He has ultimate authority over all things. His greatness is infinite.

Is God Good?

But this raises another important issue. Someone can be powerful, but that doesn't necessarily mean that he or she is good. Power isn't always a good thing. We've all witnessed people who misuse or abuse their power and authority. Some of the most powerful men in history—guys like Hitler and Stalin—have also been some of the most wicked people the world has ever encountered.

So when it comes to God, he may be all-powerful, but here's the real question: Is God good?

If you were to ask St. Paul to identify the central theme of his letter to the Romans, he would probably answer, "The righteousness of God" (Romans 1:17). Now, we've all heard the word *righteousness* before, but many of us don't know exactly what it means, especially in relation to God. Well, quite simply, righteousness refers to God's *loving faithfulness* to his people in all times and in all places. Even in the face of great difficulty—slavery, sinful rebellion, idolatry—God is always faithful to his people (even when they are not faithful to him). He promises to be with his people at all times, and he always keeps his promises.

This is very important. St. Paul wants us to know that God is not only great, but that God is also *good*. God does not use his power unjustly. God is a righteous God. He never abuses his authority. It is impossible for God to do evil or to be malicious. His power— his greatness—is always righteous and true. God never excises his sovereignty in a way that is bad or wicked. He is never unjust in his actions. God is *good*. In a word, God is *love*.

It is absolutely essential that we never forget this critical truth: *God's power is his love.* He has no power but love. And his love is all-powerful. Again, God is love—infinite love.

Unlike us humans, God will never—and can never—exercise his power unjustly or cruelly. The reason for this is simple: *God is our Father*. The *Catechism* makes sure to point out that "God's power is *loving*, for he is our Father" (CCC 268; emphasis in original). This is something that St. Paul notes at the very beginning of Romans when he is greeting his readers: "Grace to you and peace from God *our Father* (Romans 1:7; emphasis added)." And later on in Romans, St. Paul points to how blessed we are in being given the privilege of calling God, "Abba! Father!" (Romans 8:15; Galatians 4:6). We aren't just God's slaves or servants, and he is not merely our owner or master. We are nothing less than his adopted sons and daughters! We are cherished children of a heavenly Father.

The *Catechism* wants to make sure we don't miss this point. It says very clearly that "God is the *Father* Almighty, whose fatherhood and power shed light on one another" (CCC 270; emphasis in original). God's power and his fatherly love are not separate things. God's power is his love, and the fire of his love is the mightiest of all powers.

God is an almighty Father from all eternity, but it is important to remember that he is different from our own natural fathers. While human dads can sin, make mistakes, and let us down, our heavenly Father cannot—and will never—do anything unloving to his children. God is the perfect Father. In fact, human fathers should try to imitate God's perfect fatherly example (see Ephesians 3:14–15). God is the Father of *infinite* love.

God's authority, sovereignty, and power are all grounded in his perfect *fatherly* love. The Church teaches that he is a "sovereign God of love" (CCC 2628) who will never abandon his children. He will never forsake his beloved (Hebrews 13:5). He is always faithful. He can't do otherwise. Everything God does flows out of his infinite, life-giving love.

Life is not a gamble. There is no chance or randomness to our existence.

While the future may be uncertain to us, we can rest comfortably in the loving control and sovereignty of our Heavenly Father. We can trust his plan, and we can rely upon his fatherly design and control.

Why Do Bad Things Happen?

If God is so great and powerful, if he is sovereign and has ultimate authority, if nothing surprises him, then why do so many bad things still happen in the world? Wouldn't a good and powerful God want (and be able) to prevent all of the evils we witness and experience from happening?

It's easy to get confused. We learn about God's power, love, and goodness, and then we turn on the evening news and see so many things that aren't loving and good. *Where is God in all of this?*

This is something that St. Paul grappled with as well. He was not naive about the pain and suffering present in the world. In fact, he was intimately familiar with the trials that accompany life. He experienced many afflictions, endured incredible pains, and suffered tremendous disappointments (see 2 Corinthians 11:23–33). After experiencing such gruesome beatings and whippings, enduring such tremendous hardships, and suffering great loss and personal pain on numerous occasions, one would think he would be tempted to give up trust in the sovereign love of God.

But such was not the case with the apostle—far from it, actually. The same St. Paul who suffered more things in a year's time than most of us will suffer in an entire lifetime penned these words: "We know that in everything God works for good with those who love him, who are called according to his purpose" (Romans 8:28).

St. Paul totally trusted God in all circumstances and now we are called to trust him in the same way. Even while undergoing incredible pains, sufferings, and afflictions, the apostle did not waiver in his loving confidence in God's power and goodness—and we shouldn't either.

God is great. God is good. And God, in his fatherly love, has a plan for our lives that will work out for our benefit and salvation.

All we have to do is trust and obey.

GOD, THE FATHER OF MERCIES

St. Paul taught that our loving God is the Father of *mercy* (see 2 Corinthians 1:3). God is a loving, sovereign Father who knows all things and is working together to draw all men to himself (see John 12:32). Even though we have fallen into sin, God wishes to restore all of us to spiritual life and embrace us in his infinite love (see 2 Peter 3:9). He is a *merciful* Father who is so great and so good that he is able to save us fallen, sinful human beings from the clutches of death and destruction. His greatness is seen in his ability to transform our frailty and weakness into his strength and glory. His goodness is experienced in the love he showered upon us by sending his only begotten Son into the world (see Titus 3:4).

And his mercy is realized in his willingness to get his hands dirty and to continue loving us even when we appear most unlovable. Let us join the Apostle Paul in giving praise to God, "who is rich in mercy, out of the great love with which he loved us" (Ephesians 2:4). It is the mercy of God saving us from sin and death that we will begin to examine in the next chapter.

The One in Need of Answers
Who Is Man?

The Bourne trilogy has been one of the most popular movie series in the last ten years. These action-packed films tell the story of a secret agent who suffers from amnesia and can't remember anything about his past or his identity. Jason Bourne spends all of his time and risks his life in a desperate attempt to answer this question: *Who am I?*

Fortunately, we are not in the same situation as Jason Bourne. Very few, if any, of us have suffered an acute case of amnesia, and most of us have at least a general idea about our background and family. And although some of us are still in the process of self-discovery as we grow and mature, most of us have a pretty good idea of who we are and where we came from.

Nonetheless, the question we want to raise in this chapter is related to our identity: What does it mean to be human? What is our *spiritual* ancestry? Where did we come from and where are we going? In short, we want to discover our theological identity.

These are some of the most important questions we can ever ask. And there are a lot of different answers given in today's chaotic world. Some people say that we have *no* spiritual ancestry. They argue that we're just a bunch of overdeveloped organisms with no eternal significance. Others say that we are *all* gods. This second group argues that *we*—mere humans—are the source of infinite power and being. Amazing as it is, this is what many people actually believe (perhaps you've encountered some of them yourself)!

It's incredible that some people think we're merely overgrown germs with no real dignity or importance. This mentality is deadly because it leads to a tolerance of heinous practices like stem-cell manipulation, cloning, and abortion. It's equally incredible that others believe that we're really God himself—the be-all and end-all, without any need of a savior or salvation. It's easy to get confused as we wade through all of the conflicting answers to the question "What are humans?" How would the apostle Paul answer this question?

St. Paul would say that we are much more special and important than overdeveloped bacteria on the one hand, but that we are far from being almighty God on the other. He would say that we are nothing less than chosen and cherished *children of God* (see Ephesians 1:3–6). This is our identity. *We are God's adopted sons and daughters.* This is who we are. This is who we are called to be.

Who Are We (and Where Did We Come from)?
In order to help us understand our source and identity, St. Paul turns our attention to the very beginning—the creation of the world itself. The apostle encourages us to begin our investigation by studying our first parents: Adam and Eve (Romans 5:14).

One of the most famous verses in the entire Bible is Genesis 1:1. "In the beginning God created the heavens and the earth." Genesis tells the story of creation: God said "Let there be light" (Genesis 1:3), he created the animals (see Genesis 1:20–25), and he eventually made something—or, rather, *someone*—who was very special to him. In fact, this person was the most unique of all the creatures God had made...and his name was Adam.

Adam and his wife, Eve, were God's most prized earthly creatures, and he made them very different from the birds, the fish, and the trees. God made them unique. They were created in God's own *image and likeness* (see Genesis 1:26). When we say that something is like or similar to something else, we mean they have certain characteristics or traits in common. A daughter is said to be like her mother if their hair is the same color, their laugh is similar, or their smile the same angle. My car is *like* your car if we have the same model or brand or year.

Images are representations of something else. If I take a picture of a beautiful sunset, I have just captured an *image* of the sunset. The picture is not the same thing as the actual sunset itself, but it resembles and captures certain aspects of the sunset for us to see and remember even after the sunset has long passed.

This is similar to how Adam and Eve were created in relation to God. They were made in his image and likeness. That means, they resembled God in certain respects and shared a certain similarity with him. Although God is infinitely greater and more powerful than any human person, Adam and Eve still resembled him to a degree.

Adam, though much smaller and weaker and lower, was *like* God in some ways. They shared certain similarities, two of the most important similarities being *intellect and will*. God created Adam with an intellect to know truth and to understand reality. God didn't want Adam merely to live in the world; he wanted Adam to think, understand, and contemplate the things he saw and encountered. What a gift this was! God gave Adam and Eve *intellects* to understand *truth*, just as God himself has an intellect to understand the truth. Granted, God's intellect is infinitely more powerful than Adam's intellect, but his intellect still bore a certain resemblance to God's own intellect. God didn't stop there, however. He went on to give them another gift as well.

In addition to the gift of intellect, God also gave Adam and Eve *wills* with which to *love*. This is also quite remarkable. God didn't want Adam simply to be a walking calculator who could understand reality but yet have no feeling or affections for the things he encountered. He didn't want Adam to be ruled only by physical desires. God wanted people *both* to know the truth *and* to love the good—each other, and, ultimately, God himself (who is the Greatest Good).

These gifts of intellect and will were very special. The *Catechism* states that "of all visible creatures only man is 'able to know and love his Creator'" (CCC 356). Cats and dogs exist, but they can't know and love God. Birds and fish have life, but not a life that can actively worship God. We are so blessed because of all the creatures God created on this vast earth, only man "is called to share, by knowledge and love, in God's own life" (CCC 356).

And this brings us to our next point...

CREATED AS GOD'S CHILDREN

How good and generous God was to give Adam and Eve intellects to know the truth and wills to love the good! But God wanted to give them something even *more* amazing. God wanted Adam and Eve (and all their descendants) not merely to be his creatures—he wanted them to be his *adopted sons and daughters*. The greatest gift that God gave Adam and Eve—and the foundation for all of the other gifts they received—was the gift of *adoptive sonship*. The greatest gift of all was the gift of being his children.

Genesis 5:1–3 makes this point very clear. It states, "When God created man, he made him in the likeness of God" (Genesis 5:1). The Bible then says that Adam "became the father of a son in his [Adam's] own likeness, after his image, and named him Seth" (Genesis 5:3). This is vitally important: God made Adam and Eve in his own image and likeness. And, later, Adam had a son (Seth), and his son was born in Adam's image and likeness. There is an unmistakable parallel between God and Adam. As Adam came from God in God's image and likeness, so Seth came from Adam in Adam's image and likeness. Hence, in a very real sense, to be created in the "image and likeness of God" is to be God's son, just as to be born in Adam's "image and likeness" is to be Adam's son.

Having an intellect to know the truth, a will to love the good, and being God's divine children enabled Adam and Eve to live in loving relationship with each other and also with God himself (see CCC 357). Adam and Eve had a natural perfection. They lacked nothing. They had it all. They lived in a beautiful garden and had a painless life where all of their needs were met. Most importantly, however, they were "created good" and lived in "friendship" with their Creator and in "harmony" with themselves and all of the created reality around them (CCC 374).

They walked with their heavenly Father in the cool of the garden and experienced his serenity. There was no pain or suffering.

There were no marital spats between Adam and Eve. Everything was peaceful.

This type of life and existence is difficult for us to envision. Problems, pain, and suffering abound in our lives. Why was it that Adam and Eve had it so good while we have it so bad? Well, the main reason for this difference between our lives and their (initial) lives is something known as the state of *"original justice"* (see CCC 376). Because Adam was God's adopted son, he was filled with *grace* from the very beginning of his life and existence.

But what is grace? We're familiar with the hymn, "Amazing Grace," but are we sure about what this grace really is (and why it's so amazing)? The *Catechism* teaches us that grace is nothing less than our *"participation in the life of God"* himself (CCC 1997; emphasis in original). Grace is God's own being, life, and power imparted to our human souls. It is the great gift of sharing in God's own divine nature (see 2 Peter 1:4).

This makes sense when we think about our own life and family. We receive life from our parents. We receive their human nature (their humanness). This is what it means to be a father: to pass on one's nature to one's offspring. A cat passes on cat life to his kittens. A dog passes on dog life to his puppies. And a human passes on human nature and life to his babies.

In a similar way, when God created Adam and Eve as his adopted children, he also shared his own *divine life and nature* with them. From the very moment of their creation, Adam and Eve were filled with the fullness of God's grace, of his divine life and power (see CCC, 375).

The grace of God is powerful stuff! It flowed through their spiritual bloodstreams and affected every part of them, body and soul.

The grace that they received enabled them to live life free from sin and temptation. There were no sinful passions or urges in Eve. Adam didn't have to struggle with lust or irrational rage. Their intellects were fully in tune with truth and reality, and their wills were fully committed to good and loving behavior. And they had the ability to control their bodies in such a way that they never had to struggle with many of the disordered urges we have to struggle with.

All of this was in fine and proper order because they were God's children—children created in his image and likeness, children filled with his divine life and power. They were "naked and were not ashamed" (Genesis 2:25). Lust was not a problem. They had no sin in their hearts. They were totally pure. They were also *immortal*. Death was not something they were required to face. Work was easy and enjoyable for Adam and Eve. There was no pain, suffering, or struggle in their lives.

Finally, Adam and Eve—because of their close relationship with their heavenly Father—had *infused* knowledge. Learning was easy for Adam. Because of the grace and purity he possessed, Adam's intellect was more powerful than we can imagine. God gave Adam and Eve the knowledge they needed (see Sirach 17:5). In a very real sense, Adam would have made a genius like Albert Einstein look like a kindergartner.

Remember, the reason Adam and Eve had all of these super-human (or what is known as *preternatural*) gifts is because they were God's children. They had his grace—God's own divine life and being—animating and activating their own life and being. God's power flowing through their spiritual veins was the reason for the incredible abilities of their intellects, wills, and bodies. God's grace was the engine that kept everything working.

Fall from Grace

You may be getting a little frustrated as you read this. It almost feels unfair, doesn't it? Adam and Eve had it made! Everything they could ever want was practically handed to them. They had it so easy. *Why do we have it so tough? Why can't it be that easy for us, too?*

The answer to this question is a small word—only three letters— but it had a devastating effect on Adam and Eve and all who came after them (i.e., you and me). The reason for all of the problems and difficulties we now face is *sin*. Adam and Eve eventually forfeited all of their many gifts because they sinned and disobeyed the Lord.

The most important gift God gave Adam and Eve was adoptive sonship—the gift of his grace, his divine life residing within them. This was the foundation for all of the other gifts they received. Infused knowledge, painless life, and peaceful harmony were all dependent on their status as God's children. If they were to lose this grace and reject God's life, then all of the other gifts would vanish.

God warned them about this early on in their existence. Shortly after he created Adam and Eve, God gave them very clear instructions: "You may freely eat of every tree of the garden; but of the tree of the knowledge of good and evil you shall not eat, for in the day that you eat of it you shall die" (Genesis 2:16–17). Death would be the inevitable result of sin and disobedience, but this was not just any kind of death. This death would be the worst kind of death imaginable: spiritual death. The death God warned them about was the loss of his divine life animating their souls. Literally, in Hebrew (the original language of the Old Testament),

God says that they would "die" if they disobeyed. (This is not a typo—and God did not have a stuttering problem. The word is repeated twice to emphasize the seriousness of the death that would result.) This death wouldn't be small or trivial. It wouldn't even be merely physical. This death would be the worst of all deaths: It would be *spiritual*. God was telling Adam and Eve that sin was spiritual suicide.

Tragically, as we all know, Adam and Eve did not heed the Lord's warning.

They decided to put their trust in themselves rather than in God, and they fell from grace into a state of sin from which we are still recovering (see CCC 398). As soon as they ate from the tree of the knowledge of good and evil, disobeying God, they lost the divine life and grace which had so wonderfully dwelt in their souls. Their harmonious bliss was disrupted (see CCC 399).

It is important to remember that God's love did not change through this tragedy. God is love (see 1 John 4:8), and he is the same "yesterday and today and forever" (Hebrews 13:8). However, like the most malignant cancer, sin destroyed the life Adam and Eve enjoyed and extinguished the power of grace in their souls. God didn't change. Adam and Eve changed—for the worse.

Sinister Realities

What exactly is sin, anyway? Most of us grew up with a list of dos and don'ts imposed on us by our parents and teachers, and this is how many of us still understand sin today. We view it as God's rules and regulations. We are good when we do good and follow his rules. We are sinning when we break his rules and commandments.

This is true to a point. Sin, in a general sense, is anything—thought, word, or action—that offends God or violates the lawful order he has instituted. The Greek word for *sin* St. Paul uses is the word *hamartia*, which means "to miss the mark." There is a very real sense in which sin is missing, or not meeting, the expectations God has set up.

It is important to emphasize the word *miss*. Although we often think of sin as being a mark or a stain on the soul, we need to remember that sin is not *something*. Evil has no substance to it. Rather, sin is the *absence* of something that should be present. It is the lack of the love and grace that we need to survive. Sin is really *no thing*—it is nothing where there should be something. It is the absence of God's grace and love influencing our lives. We sin when we act in ways that are contrary to God's truth and love.

St. Paul begins his comments on all of this by noting that "sin came into the world through one man" (Romans 5:12). The first sin of Adam and Eve resulted in what is known as the state of *original sin*—the state of spiritual death and the loss of adoptive sonship. Spiritual death occurred the moment Adam and Eve disobeyed God. The apostle pulls no punches in noting that "death [came] through sin" (Romans 5:12). Death was not what God had in mind. It was not what he wanted for his children. And, like a deadly disease, sin and death "spread to all men" (Romans 5:12).

God wanted life for his children (see Genesis 2:7). He wanted them to have joy, happiness, and lasting and eternal pleasure. But, through and because of sin, death came into the world. The soul in which God had originally infused his life, love, and power was now empty of his divine presence. It was spiritually dead. It was hollow and empty...God's loving presence was gone. Their sin resulted in the "death of the soul" (CCC 403).

In their disobedience, Adam and Eve committed spiritual suicide. They expelled God's loving presence from their souls. They rejected the gift of divine life—the greatest and most foundational gift God had given them. The *Catechism* states that Adam and Eve immediately lost the "grace of original holiness" (CCC 399). They rejected the gift of adoptive sonship. And when this happened—when God's loving presence no longer animated their souls—everything fell apart. All the other gifts—like infused knowledge, comfort of life and immortality—were gone. Not only were they now spiritually dead, but they would also (eventually) die physically as well. From that point on, "death reigned" (Romans 5:14).

We tend to view sin as minor, insignificant. But sin is gripping. Sin is deadly. Sin enslaves. Through Adam and Eve's disobedience, we became "slaves of sin" (Romans 6:17)—slaves of death. It was our master. It reigned in our hearts. It mercilessly kept us captive, bound to death, and away from the light.

CHRIST OUR SAVIOR

Fortunately, this wasn't the end of the story. The drama of our Christian faith is not a tragedy. It is a story of reconciliation, healing, and eternal joy. There are no surprises to God. He is sovereign. He knew what was going to happen, and he had a plan to set things right...and not just right—he was going to make things infinitely better (see Genesis 3:15)!

St. Paul says that our heavenly Father knew what was coming and "chose us in him [Jesus Christ] before the foundation of the world, that we should be holy and blameless before him" (Ephesians 1:4). Did you catch that? It says that God *chose*—that he *"predestined"* (Romans 8:29)—us before the foundation of the world. This is remarkable! That means that God already had a plan for how to make things better even before you or I were blips on the cosmic radar. God had a plan even before he created Adam and Eve. God is never caught off guard. He knows all. He sees all. And he is working all things together for the good of his children (see Romans 8:28). Nothing can stop his plan of mercy and love.

St. Paul goes on:

> He destined us in love to be his sons through Jesus Christ, according to the purpose of his will, to the praise of his glorious grace which he freely bestowed on us in the Beloved. (Ephesians 1:5–6)

Hold the phone. Stop traffic. The apostle just said something that is absolutely incredible. He just made a comment that is cosmically revolutionary. Reread that passage again. Many of us have become so accustomed to hearing these verses that we almost become numb to them.

JUSTIFICATION: ADOPTED SONS IN THE ETERNAL SON

The phenomenal statement is this short phrase: "He destined us in love to be his sons *through Jesus Christ*" (Ephesians 1:5; emphasis added). Adam and Eve had it pretty good in the Garden of Eden, as we've seen. Nonetheless, as awesome as the gift of Adam and Eve's sonship was, it doesn't begin to compare with the sonship of God's *Eternal Son*. Adam was God's son by grace. The Eternal Son (Jesus) is God's Son because he's "eternally begotten of the

Father." *He is God himself!* Everything that the Father has (and is) has been given to the Son. The Son is one in being with the Father. Thus, his divine sonship is infinitely more glorious, splendorous, and incredible than Adam's sonship for this very simple reason: the Eternal Son of God *is* God!

Another incredible thing is that we don't merely go back or return to the type of sonship that Adam and Eve had from the beginning. No. As cool as that might sound, St. Paul tells us that we now receive an even greater sonship—we receive *sonship through Jesus himself.* Our heavenly Father loved us so much that he gave us an incredible gift that is even more powerful and glorious than the gift he gave Adam and Eve at the very beginning.

God gave us himself: Jesus. And Jesus himself gives us to his Father.

This teaching is called the doctrine of *justification.* The *Catechism* states that through our baptism we participate in the "grace of Christ" (CCC 1997). Baptism is the sacrament that unites us to Jesus. In baptism we become one with him (see Romans 6:3–4). And as sons and daughters of God in the Eternal Son of God, we can "call God 'Father,' in union with the only Son" (CCC 1997).

We have received a grace and blessing even more beautiful than the gift received by Adam and Eve: We are now sons and daughters of God *with and in* the Eternal Son of God. One of the greatest councils in the history of the Catholic Church defined justification as a "translation from that state in which man is born a child of the first Adam, to the state of grace and of the adoption of the sons of God through the second Adam, Jesus Christ, our Savior."[5] When we are justified, we are *declared* and *made* divinely adopted sons and daughters of God (see 1 John 3:1). This doctrine of adoptive sonship is at the heart of the Catholic understanding of justification.

St. Paul says that Jesus is the new and second Adam (see Colossians 3). Where Adam failed, Jesus succeeded. Where Adam sinned, Jesus obeyed (see Luke 22:42). Where Adam died in sin, Christ rose to life in glory (see Romans 6:4). And the life that Adam lost in sin, the Eternal Son has given us even more abundantly in love.

We recognize that our Protestant brothers and sisters have a different understanding of the doctrine of justification. But since we can't go into exhaustive detail here, we've decided to limit our discussion to the Catholic understanding (which we believe is most consistent with the writings of St. Paul).

THE GOSPEL

The Gospel, the good news of our faith (Romans 1:1–6) is what St. Paul spent his life preaching. It is the good news of Jesus Christ, and the hope we have to be children of God with and in him. "The wages of sin is death, but the free gift of God is eternal life in Christ Jesus our Lord" (Romans 6:23).

Of all the promises and gifts that God could give us, nothing compares with the glory and splendor of being his divinely adopted children *in Jesus*. This is something we could never earn (see CCC 2007) in the same way we can't work our way into someone's family. We can't pay someone to make us his children—being a son or a daughter (even of a human family) is a priceless gift. Nothing we could ever do on our own would obligate God to make us members of his divine family. He does so purely out of his love and mercy (see CCC 2008).

We are sons and daughters who can rely upon our heavenly Father in all things. We have a merciful Father who is willing to take us by the hand and dust us off when we slip and fall. Our Father never grows tired of hearing our little voices speak to him in prayer—no matter what time it is—and he will never tune us out—no matter how stupid we think we sound. No need or request is too great for him to fulfill. He's got the whole world—and every aspect of our lives—in the palm of his loving hands. He never rejects his children when they call. He never abandons us in our weakness. In fact, it is when we are most weak, and are forced to rely upon him, that we are most strong (see 2 Corinthians 12:10).

"God shows his love for us in that while we were yet sinners"— sinners who had rejected the gift of adoptive sonship—"Christ died for us" (Romans 5:8). What incredible love and amazing grace! How glorious it is that, when we were so lost and distant, Jesus came to earth and died so that we might live with and in him.

It is from the cross that we receive his life-giving love. It is through the cross that we have faith in his mercy. The eternal Son of God came to earth, lived, died, and rose again so that we might "obtain the glorious liberty of the children of God" (Romans 8:21). Jesus came to set us free. He came to liberate us from slavery to sin (see Romans 6:7) so that we could embrace the loving bond of righteousness (see Romans 6:18).

For all who are led by the Holy Spirit of God are sons of God. For you did not receive the spirit of slavery to fall back into fear, but you have received the spirit of sonship. When we cry, 'Abba, Father!' it is the Spirit himself bearing witness with our spirit that we are children of God, and if children, then heirs, heirs of God and fellow heirs with Christ. (Romans 8:14–17)

This is the Gospel—the good news—that Jesus made possible for and in us. What a gift this is! What a life which is ours to live! And what an identity we have received!

CHAPTER THREE

Words Cannot Express
How God and Man Relate

There is probably no more famous verse in the Bible than John 3:16:

> For God so loved the world that he gave his only Son, so that whoever believes in him should not perish but have eternal life.

It's on bumper stickers and billboards, coffee cups and T-shirts, and even on poster boards in every end zone of every football game. It's so popular, in part, because most Christians feel that it sums up the whole story of salvation.

It is a powerful and straightforward verse, one that St. Paul assuredly would have agreed with and preached on often. There is one word in the verse, however, that the devil can sometimes twist to confuse us—the word *world*.

We can sometimes think that this means that God doesn't think of us personally, but only collectively. And while God does absolutely think of us as one body, which we'll discuss more later, it's important—no, make that *essential*—to understand that God thinks of us and loves us personally, too. Yes, God so loved the world, but how differently does the verse read when we make it personal? Try it:

> For God so loved *me* that he gave his only Son, that *I would believe* in him, would not perish, and have eternal life.

For St. Paul, it was personal. It should be for us, too. Although God does relate to us in cosmic ways and worldly events, he is intimately connected to us. Even if God knew that every other living being until the end of time would reject his love, he still would have mounted that cross and died, just for you. Paul believed this, and his preaching showed it.

Sometimes it's difficult for us to grasp the truth about how and why God became man, but the Incarnation (Latin for "made flesh") is vital for us to understand as we move forward. The Incarnation, when God took flesh and "dwelt among us" (John 1:14), is a mystery, but it is a mystery to be meditated upon, not solved. Too often it creates conflict within us because we approach it strictly intellectually, with our minds, and don't allow our hearts to get involved. We need mind and heart, however, if we wish to understand how God relates to man, for God gave us all three, and he calls us to give all three back to him (see Deuteronomy 6:5; Matthew 22:37).

The Incarnation—It's Not for the Birds

I remember the first time that this truth of God become man really came to life in my own mind and heart simultaneously. I heard a story that really changed the way I looked at the Incarnation—a simple story, often shared around Christmastime. It was made famous by radio celebrity Paul Harvey, and here is an excerpt from his broadcast.

There was a kind, decent, mostly good man. Generous to his family, upright in his dealings with other men. But he just didn't believe all that Incarnation stuff that the churches proclaim at Christmastime. He just couldn't swallow the Jesus Story, about God coming to earth as a man. "I'm not going with you to church this Christmas Eve." He told his wife, stating that he'd feel like a hypocrite. And so he stayed and his family went to the midnight service.

Shortly after the family drove away, snow began to fall. He watched the flurries getting heavier and then went back to his fireside chair to read his newspaper. Minutes later he was startled by a thudding sound.... Then another. Sort of a thump or a thud.... At first he thought someone must be throwing snowballs against his living room window. But when he went to the front door to investigate he found a flock of birds huddled miserably in the snow. They'd been caught in the storm and, in a desperate search for shelter, had tried to fly through his large landscape window. Well, he couldn't let the poor creatures lie there and freeze, so he remembered the barn where his children stabled their pony. That would provide a warm shelter, if he could direct the birds to it.

Quickly he put on a coat and tramped through the deepening snow to the barn. He opened the doors wide and turned on a light, but the birds did not come in. So he hurried back to the house, fetched bread crumbs, sprinkled them on the snow, making a trail to the yellow-lighted wide open doorway of the stable. But to his dismay, the birds ignored the bread crumbs, and continued to flap around helplessly in the snow. He tried catching them.... He tried shooing them into the barn by walking around them waving his arms.... Instead, they scattered in every direction, except into the warm, lighted barn. And then, he realized that they were afraid of him. To them, he reasoned, I am a strange and terrifying creature.

If only I could think of some way to let them know that they can trust me... That I am not trying to hurt them, but to help them. But how? Any move he made tended to frighten them, confuse them. They just would not follow. They would not be led because they feared him. *If only I could be a bird,* he thought, *and mingle with them and speak their language. Then I could tell them not to be afraid. Then I could show them the way to the safe, warm barn. But I would have to be one of them so they could see, and hear and understand.*

At that moment the church bells began to ring. He stood there listening to the bells, playing "Adeste Fidelis" and pealing the glad tidings of Christmas. And he sank to his knees in the snow.[6]

This story has been read and shared countless times over the years, in books and on radio shows, in newspapers and on television programs, in almost every imaginable language. Why? Sure, it's a good story, but what makes the story so popular? Is it because we all have loved ones who we wish were more into their faith? Is it because we've all questioned the existence of God before and wondered if he really cares about us personally? Or is it that we are fascinated by how God, the unmoved mover and uncreated creator, makes his presence known to us? The question demands an answer, an answer you probably already know.

In the Flesh

Why did God become man? Why did the Word become flesh?

You know the answer. There is a line in the Nicene Creed that we pray each week at Mass: "Begotten, not made, consubstantial with the Father; through him, all things were made. For us men and for our salvation, he came down from heaven." That's the short answer to the question. That's why God became man. God became man for our salvation. God is love, and *true love* works for the salvation of the beloved.

So, *what* are we supposed to learn from Christ in the New Testament that we couldn't or didn't learn about God before Christ's birth in the Old Testament? These were the questions that Paul, an educated and respected Pharisee, had to come to terms with in his own life. St. Paul explained it to the people in Philippi like this:

> Christ Jesus, who, though he was in the form of God, did not count equality with God a thing to be grasped, but emptied himself, taking the form of a servant, being born in the likeness of men. And being found in human form he humbled himself and became obedient unto death, even death on a cross. (Philippians 2:5–8)

These words contain very deep truths. God became what we are to give us what he is; he came down to us so that we could get back up to him. Through the Incarnation, God meets us where we are, walking and pointing us to where we need to go. In Christ Jesus, we have a God who is not afraid to get his hands dirty.

The Incarnation is simultaneously a simple truth and a profound mystery, a beautiful and joyful mystery. Our Church unpacks this truth even further in the *Catechism* (456–463), offering us four distinct reasons why God emptied himself and took on flesh in Christ Jesus.

He came to *reconcile* us with God.

He came that we might know God's *love.*

He came to model *holiness.*

He came so that we could become "partakers in the *divine nature.*"

These four truths offer a very different perspective of God than most people in St. Paul's day were used to, Paul included. When he came face-to-face with Jesus, everything changed. The God St. Paul thought he knew wasn't who God really was at all. Paul immediately became aware of his own sinfulness and the need he had for a savior. That's what the Gospel should do for us, today, too. The Gospel comforts the afflicted, yes, but the Gospel should also afflict us when we're too comfortable. Paul got a wake-up call, and the Gospel did for him what it has been doing for individuals ever since; it offered him the unparalleled gift of self-awareness.

Self-Awareness: The Key to True Holiness

The good news of God's forgiveness is often not seen as being very good in modern culture. In a modern culture that doesn't really believe in sin, what good is forgiveness? Why do we need a doctor if we're not sick? Why would I need a Savior, since if it feels right, I must not be sinning?

The Gospel is good news because it contains not only the bad news about sin, but also the good news about salvation. The Gospel (and all of Scripture) is inspired by the Holy Spirit, whom Benedict XVI referred to as "the soul of our soul."[7] It's in this way that our soul is moved by the words (and works) of sacred Scripture. The same way a baby responds to his or her parents' voice long before they can understand the actual words being spoken, our souls respond, even leap (see Luke 1:41) when the Holy Spirit breathes truth into us. Through reading and, more to the point, *living* the Gospel, the Holy Spirit invites us to heightened new levels of self-awareness.

This newfound self-awareness necessitates a decision on our part in answer to the following question: "Am I going to continue to live for myself (Adam), or am I going to surrender my life and live for God (Christ)?" Every decision in life offers you a choice to be like Adam in Eden and to put yourself first, or like Christ in Gethsemane and choose the Church—two gardens, two choices, two drastically different results. Paul explains this in great detail in chapters five and six of his letter to the Romans.

If we recognize our sin and are humble enough to admit it, the decision is quite easy. The Gospel helps us both to admit sin and to live humbly. If we were writing this out in steps, it might look something like this:

Step One: Encounter the Gospel.
Step Two: Realize there is a God.
Step Three: Admit that it is not you.
Step Four: Acknowledge that Christ is God.
Step Five: Admit that you are a sinner.
Step Six: Realize that you need a Savior.
Step Seven: Repent and be reconciled to God.
Step Eight: Believe the Gospel.
Step Nine: Change the way you live.
Step Ten: Share the Gospel with others.

Our awareness of God's sovereignty and mercy coupled with our new awareness of our own incredible pride and sinfulness leads us to an incredible decision.

To Repent or Not to Repent—That Is the Question

Many believe that repentance means telling God you're sorry. That definition is not incorrect, but it's also not complete. Let's take a deeper look.

While repentance is a movement of the heart and not a strictly logical decision, sometimes it helps to approach it in more logical terms. Imagine repentance as a 180-degree turn. Picture yourself standing in a hallway, gazing down the corridor. You're staring into darkness; behind you is a bright light. As you turn your body ninety degrees, darkness is now on your left and brightness on your right. The ninety-degree turn that puts darkness and light into your peripheral vision is the first half of repentance: turning away from darkness (sin). You still have a way to go, however; it's not enough to stand still between the two. You must keep moving toward the light.

Incidentally, this is where most people get stuck during the sacrament of reconciliation. It's in this movement that the heart and mind can sometimes fall into conflict. If, for instance, you've ever confessed a sin because you feared the consequences but weren't really, heartily sorry for the sin, you got stuck in the hallway and didn't complete the turn. For the sacrament to be valid, for your sins to be absolved, and for grace to really take root, you must be truly *contrite*.

What does *contrite* mean? Contrite comes from a Latin word meaning "worn down." Basically, when we've been worn down by our guilt and our sin, and we wholeheartedly and humbly admit our wrongdoing with remorse and penitence, we are contrite. The Church offers us guidance, providing us with a prayer called the *Act of Contrition*. Part of that prayer is us begging God for the grace and strength not only to avoid our sins in the future, but to avoid the *environments, relationships,* and *occasions* that lead to those sins.

Repentance is the proper (and humble) response to that new self-awareness mentioned earlier. It's only with the help of God's grace and a truly penitent (repentant) and humbled heart that you can make that second ninety-degree turn toward the light of Christ. When you make that second movement toward the light, you are consumed by God's grace, which allows you to live out your life in amazing ways.

Virtue-all Reality: Staying Focused on the Light

The Incarnation is how the timeless one entered time and space, in human form, emptying himself (Philippians 2:7) to become like us in all things, "yet without sin" (Hebrews 4:15). *This is how God relates to man:* through Jesus Christ, the "one mediator between God and man" (1 Timothy 2:5). It is through Jesus that we are now justified, as we discussed in the last chapter. But what does justification look like on a daily basis? How does that change the way God and I relate, much less the way I live day to day? How do I protect my state of grace, live a contrite life, and allow Christ's light to shine through me?

Put very simply, once justified, God now endows us with virtues to help us become more like Christ. Most specifically, Paul points to the three theological virtues of faith, hope, and love (1 Corinthians 13:13) as the greatest gifts that God bestows upon those who are justified. But how does this work?

Through the Incarnation, God blesses us with adoptive sonship:

> God sent forth his Son, born of woman, born under the law,
> so that we might receive adoption as sons. And because you
> are sons, God has sent the Spirit of his Son into our hearts,
> crying, 'Abba! Father!' So through God you are no longer a
> slave but a son, and if a son, then an heir. (Galatians 4:4–7)

Now, through the grace of adoptive sonship, we are enabled to live out the virtues. A chapter later in St. Paul's same Letter to the Galatians, he lists several of the virtues as fruit of the Holy Spirit: "the fruit of the Spirit is love, joy, peace, patience, kindness, goodness, faithfulness, gentleness, and self-control" (Galatians 5:22–23).

But what exactly is a virtue, and how does it work?

Virtue comes from the Latin word *virtus*, meaning "excellence." Its root is *vir* (Latin for "man"). Virtues are the way in which man reaches his highest excellence or moral perfection. All virtues are founded on the greatest virtue: love. While there are dozens of virtues, there are seven that receive the greatest amount of attention in Catholic teachings. We've already mentioned the theological virtues of faith, hope, and love. In addition, the cardinal virtues are temperance (moderation), prudence, justice, and fortitude. Out of these seven come other virtues like chastity, humility, and patience.

A virtue is a habitual and firm disposition to do what is good. In other words, to be all that you are called (and designed) to be by God your Father (Matthew 5:48), you have to tap into and unleash the power of God's grace within you, by virtue of the virtues. Virtues are acquired and strengthened by the repetition of morally good acts. The virtues, like muscles, become stronger with exercise.

THE BIG THREE

St. Gregory of Nyssa said, "The goal of a virtuous life is to become like God."[8] That is exactly the point St. Paul was trying to make in the fifth chapter of Romans.

> Therefore, since we are justified by faith, we have peace with God through our Lord, Jesus Christ. Through Him we have obtained access to this grace in which we stand, and we rejoice in our hope of sharing the glory of God. More than that, we rejoice in our sufferings, knowing that suffering produces endurance, and endurance produces character, and character produces hope, and hope does not disappoint us, because God's love has been poured into our hearts through the Holy Spirit that has been given to us. (Romans 5:1–5)

Now, if you got lost reading that, don't feel bad. The book of Romans is one of the most poetic, beautifully written, and often complex of any of the books of the Bible. Each verse contains a lot of depth, so don't feel bad if you need to read a passage more than once. Let's break this one down into a few pieces.

"Therefore, since we are justified by faith, we have peace with God through our Lord, Jesus Christ" (Romans 5:1; emphasis added). Remember, being justified brings with it the big three theological virtues of faith, hope, and love. This verse shows us that, by faith, we have access to God, and we will live at peace with him. It's not just having faith that he is real; it's the faith that he loves us and is behind us, cheering us on to heaven. It's knowing that the grace we need to get there is available to us, at all times.

"Through him we have obtained access to this grace in which we stand, and we rejoice in our hope of sharing the glory of God... and hope does not disappoint" (Romans 5:2, 5; emphasis added). This verse reminds us that God keeps his promises. That's what hope is—believing in God's promises for you. God is trustworthy and he promises great things for those who live for him.

> More than that, we rejoice in our sufferings, knowing that suffering produces endurance, and endurance, produces character, and character produces hope, and hope does not disappoint us, because God's love has been poured into our hearts through the Holy Spirit that has been given to us. (Romans 5:3–5)

When we live a virtuous life, especially in the face of suffering, we demonstrate true love, which comes from the Holy Spirit's presence in our hearts. Notice, too, that virtue helps us endure suffering, and it builds character.

Did you notice how faith, hope, and love are all *active?* Virtues aren't philosophical or theoretical; virtues are practical and tangible. What is even cooler is that the virtues within us are purified (and elevated) by divine grace (see CCC 1804–1839), meaning that, through God's grace, the virtues can literally transform us from sinners into saints. You might be thinking, *okay, that sounds nice in theory, but how does it work practically, and what do the virtues have to do with God?*

GRACE: THE ULTIMATE TRANSFORMER

Grace is God's life, God's very life, in us. Grace is how God makes us more like him. Grace powers virtue. Grace is how God *transforms* us. This is not to imply that we are like science fiction

Transformers who change from one thing to another and then back again. No, the hope of grace is that we change for the better, for good. God doesn't just want to transform our outer appearance, like a robot in a movie. No, God wishes to transform us from the inside out. "Grace is God leaning forward and stooping towards man."[9] Grace is how we truly become "partakers in the divine nature" (2 Peter 3:1). Grace undoes what was done in Eden, but it also extends to us who God is in heaven.

Adam's sin led us into slavery, and Christ's redemption led us out. Paul explains this in detail, showing the parallels and contrasts between Adam and Jesus (see Romans 5:12–21). Both lives had a huge impact on the world, but the similarities really end there. As Paul puts it, "[though] one man's trespass led to condemnation for all men, so one man's act of righteousness leads to acquittal and life for all men" (Romans 5:18). Paul taught that the grace of Christ more than makes up for the sin of Adam. The power of grace is unparalleled and unstoppable. He even goes on to say that "where sin increased, grace abounded all the more" (Romans 5:20).

This means that no matter how much we sin, God's grace is always there in abundance. As Paul reminded the people in Corinth, "[God's] grace is sufficient," and his "power is made perfect in weakness" (2 Corinthians 12:9).

DROWNING IN SIN OR DROWNING IN GRACE?
In effect, God is saying, "Don't be overwhelmed by sin. As much sin as you may be immersed in, there is always more grace. I've got you covered." And grace doesn't just cover us—it consumes us. At some point we might wonder, though, *If God's grace gets poured out so much when we sin, why not just sin more and release a*

whole bunch of God's grace? That idea is rooted in reverse logic and, as error-filled as it is, it's not a new way of thinking. St. Paul dealt with similar thinking, and he warned the people in Rome against it.

> Are we to continue in sin that grace may abound? By no means! How can we who died to sin still live in it? Do you not know that all of us who were baptized into Christ Jesus were baptized into his death? We were buried therefore with him by Baptism into death, so that as Christ was raised from the dead by the glory of God the Father, we too might walk in newness *of* life. (Romans 6:1–4)

Here, Paul makes it very clear that the very purpose of grace is not only to forgive us of past sins but to assist us in our efforts to avoid future *sins*. In the sacrament of confession, grace pours out and overflows in absolution for just this reason. The sacraments—all of them—were instituted by Christ himself as outward signs that bring *grace.*

In baptism, we die to sin and are freed from its bondage. Sin no longer has power over us. One of the elements and symbols at baptism is water. Our bodies are composed mainly of water. We can live longer without food than we can without water. Get the idea? We need water to live, but baptism is about a lot more than water.

Some people have the mistaken idea that the waters of baptism are just about washing away original sin. Yes, they do that, but it's about so much more than that. Baptism doesn't just erase sin; it destroys death, and it welcomes you into the family. Through baptism you are not cleaned off, you are recreated. In the sacrament of baptism, we are made new; we are joined to Christ. Our sins are put to death, and our souls are filled with life. In this way, the physical *sign of water* represents death to our old life and rising in a new life. Every time we bless ourselves with holy water, it should remind us of when we received the reality (not merely the symbol) of new life in Christ at our baptism. When we bless ourselves upon entering the Church, we renew our baptismal vows, vowing to die to the philosophies and mistruths of the world and to live only for God.

Can you imagine how different our Church and our world would be if we *really embraced* the truth, importance, and beauty of baptism, beyond thinking of it as a ceremony or a cute little baby in a white dress? St. Paul wanted everyone to understand the intense and amazing ramifications of what occurs at baptism, so he reminded us: "So you also must consider yourselves dead to sin and alive to God in Christ Jesus" (Romans 6:11).

Christ's didn't just die for our past sins. He died (and rose) that you and I might die to sin (present and future) and fully live (present and future) for and with God. As we mentioned in the first chapter, creation naturally reflects and points back to its creator. Our bodies and, indeed, our very lives are arrows that point to the source of our life. It is God who created us, and it is God whom we are designed to reflect. If God gave us the gift of our bodies and souls to serve as arrows that point others back to him, will we use our bodies for his glory or for sin (see Romans 6:12–14 and CCC 2819)?

Is Your Master a Who or a What?

It was the 1800s and a young miner who had recently struck it rich in the gold rush was on his way back East. As he stopped in

New Orleans to rest, he noticed a crowd of people gathering for some kind of event.

He approached the crowd and quickly learned they were there for a slave auction. He heard a gavel bang on wood and a man exclaim, "Sold!" just as a middle-aged black man was taken away.

Next, a beautiful young black girl was pushed onto the platform and made to walk around so everyone could see her. The miner heard vile jokes and comments that spoke of evil intentions from those around him. The bidding began. Within a minute (because of her beauty), the bids surpassed what most slave owners would pay for a black girl. Finally, one man bid a price that was beyond the reach of the other. The girl looked down.

The auctioneer called out, "Going once! Going twice!"

Just before the final call, the miner yelled out a price that was exactly twice the previous bid, an amount that exceeded the worth of any man.

The crowd laughed. The miner opened up the bag of gold he had brought for the trip. The auctioneer shook his head in disbelief as he waved the girl over to him. The girl walked down the steps of the platform until she was eye-to-eye with the miner. She spat straight in his face and said through clenched teeth, "I hate you!"

The miner, without a word, wiped his face, paid the auctioneer, took the girl by the hand, and walked away from the still-laughing crowd.

Stretching out his hand, he said to the girl, "Here are your manumission papers." The girl looked at the papers, then looked at him, and looked at the papers once again.

"You just bought me...and now, you're setting me free?"

"That's why I bought you. I bought you to set you free."

The beautiful young girl fell to her knees in front of the miner, tears streaming down her face.

"You bought me to set me free! You bought me to set me free!" she said over and over. The miner said nothing. Clutching his muddy boots, the girl looked up at the miner and said, "All I want to do is to serve you—because you bought me to set me free!"[10]

It's an imperfect analogy, as all analogies regarding God's infinite and perfect love are, but it does demonstrate some sound principles regarding human nature. The point we must take and ask ourselves, however, is the point St. Paul was getting at, namely: "Who is your master, and why do you serve him?" He sounds a lot like Christ in Matthew 6:24.

Sincerely ask yourself whether you serve God. When you are deciding what to do this weekend, are you seeking to please God or yourself? When you are deciding how far to go with the people you date, how much to drink, whether or not to look at pornography, or what to wear, who has the deciding vote—you or God? Who is the *true* master of your life, God or sin?

Paul is asking a difficult question and it deserves an honest response. He is reminding us that God died and rose for us so that we would love and serve him. It wouldn't make sense to have a new master purchase you and still work for the old master, would it? We were purchased with the blood of Christ (1 Corinthians 6:20; 7:23). Rising with Christ means that God is our new master, the one who loves us and has freed us. He is the one whom we ought to serve—out of love. That's what St. Paul's talking about when he writes:

Do you not know that if you yield yourselves to any one as obedient slaves, you are slaves of the one whom you obey, either of sin which leads to death, or of obedience, which leads to righteousness? But thanks be to God that you who were once slaves of sin have become obedient from the heart...and having been set free from sin, have become slaves of righteousness. (Romans 6:16–18)

Sin might sound fun at times. Sin might feel good at times. But, ultimately, all sin does is kill you. St. Paul was so clear on this point that he offered one of the most clear yet startling verses recorded in the Bible: "The wages of sin is death." If the master you serve is sin, the payment for your services will be your death.

So, what is the cure for death? The answer lies in the rest of the verse: "For the wages of sin is death, but the free gift of God is eternal life in Christ Jesus our Lord" (Romans 6:23). Eternal life is the cure for death, and how do we obtain eternal life? Grace. St. Paul, then, understood the transformative power of grace and the need we all have for it. Grace offers us true freedom and true life...a new life.

Don't Just Be a Good Person—Be a Christian

One of the greatest modern lies is that Christianity is about being a nice person. Countless masses of Christians, Catholics included, think that living as a Christian means not rocking the boat, being polite, and keeping the peace at all costs. This leaves no room for authentic love, because an indispensable part of love is truth. Rather than saying what needs to be said, many modern Christians proclaim the gospel of nice to avoid upsetting close friends at school or family members around the Thanksgiving dinner table. That approach, however, is not consistent with the Gospel (see Luke 12:53). One modern Catholic writer put it this way: [from Blessed are the Bored—reword]

> The harsh truth is that Jesus isn't calling you to be a good person. Jesus Christ is calling you to be a *new* person, a new creation (Galatians 2:20), not just converted in mind but transformed in body and spirit. That means admitting that the life you currently lead might not be the life you're called to lead. It means acknowledging that there are areas of your life in which you won't let the Lord be the Lord.[11]

Living as a new creation means that we "hate and avoid sin now *not out of fear of punishment* (the former motive) and *not simply out of gratitude* (Luther's answer, but not St. Paul's) but we avoid sin *because of who we are, Christ's.*"[12] One could say "I avoid sin because it's just not me." We belong to Christ. We are "little Christs," as St. Augustine would say. Love is what unites us to him, not obedience or fear, but authentic love. We are connected by the power of his love. In the authentic, selfless love of Jesus, we allow him to be far more than just our healer, teacher, or miracle worker—he is our Savior. Jesus Christ didn't just save us from the punishment for sin, he saved us from sin itself, so that we would never again have to be mastered by it. Love is what conquers sin.

To recap, *this is how God and man relate.* God wants man to become more like God and get back to him. He shares the good news (the Gospel) with us about Jesus Christ and his resurrection. The good news, in turn, demands a response from us, and the wise (and humble) response is repentance. Once we repent we need to seek out God's grace, beginning with baptism, and become more aware of the sin that binds us and pushes out God's grace. We must respond to our newfound freedom in Christ by living out our identity as new creations in Christ. As new creations, we ought to work for salvation, as he does, avoiding sin, speaking truth, and putting our faith into action. Living as Christ also implies that our faith will be active—that it will inspire works born out of love.

Again, you might be saying to yourself (as those in Paul's day probably said), "I really do want to live for Christ, but what happens when I'm not at church, at a conference, at a camp, or on retreat? What happens when I'm coming down from the mountain, and I'm not surrounded by my friends who believe the same things I do? What happens when I am at work and I'm the odd one out, with no community of support? What happens when I am forced to face those same relationships, environments, and temptations to sin and my retreat high is gone?"

St. Paul knew you'd ask that, too. That's why his advice is so practical and so timely, even today, and we'll find out why in the next chapter

CHAPTER FOUR

Losing the Fake I.D.
How Man Relates to Himself

In chapter one we examined a well-known mealtime prayer. However, as famous as this prayer may be, there is another prayer that is even more famous. And while this particular prayer doesn't rhyme like the mealtime grace, it carries a certain power and depth with which no other prayer can even begin to compete. The reason for this is simple: *It came from the lips of our Savior himself.* Without a doubt, the most famous prayer of all time is the Our Father.

We say the Our Father at each and every Mass. It is beautiful, mystical, and personal. It is deep and, to be perfectly honest, a little perplexing, too. There are certain parts of the Our Father which just don't seem to fit what we would expect in the Christian life.

The prayer starts off simply enough: "Our Father, who art in heaven, hallowed be your name," and it goes on to ask that the Lord's kingdom come, that his will be accomplished, and that our needs be met. So far so good. But the puzzling part comes near the end: "Lead us not into temptation, but deliver us from evil."

Whoa! "Lead us not into temptation"? Why do we need to *ask* for this? Isn't it a given?

WHY ARE WE STILL TEMPTED?

One of the most troubling things new Christians face is the persistent reality of sin in their lives. Some people experience a deep and profound conversion to Christ, return to the Church and the sacraments with renewed vigor, and commit themselves to a life of holiness and truth. Their hearts are on fire with love for God. Other people might come back from a retreat or conference overflowing with joy, feeling as though Christ's presence is radiating from their very pores. They then reenter the routine of their day-to-day lives, and eventually, as time goes on, they notice that their spiritual passion begins to diminish. The light slowly fades. The sparkle begins to dull. And they are confronted with the same sins, struggles, and temptations they faced before their conversion.

This can be incredibly discouraging. Sometimes people even question whether they had a real or authentic encounter with God at all. Perhaps they just imagined everything. Maybe it wasn't as powerful as they had originally thought. Surely if they had *truly* encountered Jesus Christ, sin and temptation would stop being a problem, right?

Well...not exactly. As nice as it would be, sin and temptation remain a constant battle even after a conversion to Christ. Jesus knew this would be the case, and that is why he instructed us to ask for divine help in avoiding the lure of evils that surround us. "Lead us not into temptation" is not a trivial request; our Lord wants us to make this a petition from the bottom of our hearts. Temptation is real...even for the Christian. One could argue *especially* for the Christian. Like it or not, the battle against sin is a battle we will fight our entire lives.

SINNER-SAINTS

It can be frustrating to read through the Bible. We learn about so many people of great faith, and we grow discouraged when we compare our lives to theirs. Most of us haven't raised anyone from the dead, cast out demons, or miraculously cured the sick. Far from it—most of us struggle with depression, boredom, lust, and lukewarmness. It almost seems unfair. Everyone in the Bible is doing great things with deep faith...and we're doing jack! It just seems to come so easy to them.

Why can't holiness be that easy for all of us?

Well, it may surprise you, but the simple truth of the matter is *that it really wasn't all that easy for the people in the Bible to follow God, either.* Yes, the biblical saints had profound encounters with the grace of God, but they also had profound difficulties to work through too. Everyone (but Jesus and Mary) had to struggle with the reality of sin and temptation in their lives.

Even St. Paul.

St. Paul might seem almost like a super apostle, always proclaiming the truth, converting people to Christ, and performing miracles. But St. Paul struggled with sin and temptation just like you and I. And this isn't something we have to figure out or deduce on our own. St. Paul admits it himself.

Speaking about all people of all generations, the apostle describes the tension between good and evil that we all face. Grace is real, it is powerful. It saves—transforming fallen sons of Adam into beloved sons of God (Romans 5:12–15; 1 Corinthians 15:22,

45)—but the fight is still real. Sin is still present. Temptation must still be resisted.

Romans 7:15 says something to which we can all relate: "I do not understand my own actions. For I do not do what I want, but I do the very thing I hate."

St. Paul understands the struggles we face. There are times when sin seems to overpower us. We want to follow Jesus, we want to abandon ourselves to the power of his love and grace, but the flashy lights of the world feel too great for us to resist...and we fall. This can be a very painful experience for the Christian. Here we are, baptized followers of Christ, striving to obey his commandments, desperately seeking the peace of his healing touch, and yet sin remains. We still have to go to confession; we still have to fight against the "old nature" (Ephesians 4:22–24)— the bad habits and addictions that still plague us.

There are times when we almost feel like spiritual schizophrenics—like religious Dr. Jekylls and Mr. Hydes. We know that sin is deadly. We know that Christ is our only hope for lasting joy and happiness. We believe what the Bible says and what the Church teaches, and yet we still stumble and fall. Our bodies, passions, and disordered desires drive us away from holiness, and we land painfully in sin.

The battle between good and evil isn't just fought out there in the world around us. No, the battle is also fought in here, *within* ourselves, and it is literally a fight between supernatural life and death.

St. Paul understood this battle we all face. He said it was almost like there was "another law at war with the law of my mind and making me captive to the law of sin which dwells in my members"

(Romans 7:23). We know the truth with our mind—we sincerely "delight in the law of God" in our inmost being (see Romans 7:22)—but our fleshly appetites urge us to do the very things we despise. It is immortal combat in the most literal sense of the phrase. It is a war for our very souls.

Fighting the Inner Fight

The "inclination towards sin" that we all experience is called *concupiscence*. It is the almost involuntary urge we feel towards sinful thoughts and actions. The *Catechism* says that although baptism has cleansed us with a forgiveness that is "full and complete," we still have to face the "weakness of human nature." Our humanity is still susceptible to the lure of temptation and sin. Hence, "we must still combat the movements of concupiscence that never cease leading us to evil" (CCC 978). Concupiscence, the "inclination to evil" (CCC 405), which everyone (but Jesus and Mary) has to face, "makes man's life a battle" (CCC 409). We are at war with the forces of evil. Thus, we must stand firm in Christ our Savior and resist the pull of sin in our lives.

St. Paul echoes the painful cry many of us feel deep down in our bones as we fight temptations: "Wretched man that I am! Who will deliver me from this body of death?" (Romans 7:24). Again, the answer is Jesus: "Christ Jesus has set me free from the law of sin and death" (Romans 8:2). Jesus Christ is the only one who can free us from the power of sin. We must run to him.

Our Only Hope

"What can I do about this?" you may ask. "I'm trying to follow Jesus with all of my heart, but I just can't seem to stay away from the pull of sin. You don't understand how hard it is. Pornography, drugs, alcohol, illicit sex, gambling, stealing, gossiping, lying—all of these things just have a grip on me. I've been trying to fight sin, but I can't break the power it has over me. I just can't do it."

There are several things that can be said in response to this very real plea for help. First of all, yes, as hard as it may be to believe, *we do understand how hard it is.* We understand the reality of the fight against sin. We struggle the same way you do. It's not easy for anyone to live in this materialistic and pornographic culture of death. Each morning we have to get up and beg the Lord for the grace and strength to fight the world, the flesh, and the devil, just like you.

Trust us, temptation and sin is very real to us as well. We have fight like anyone else—and, sadly, sometimes we fall. And this brings us to our next point.

You're right: You—we—can't do it. We'll lose every time. But there is hope. This battle can be won! Immediately after St. Paul mourns the pull of sin, he raises his hands to heaven and praises our heavenly Father for the hope he has given us: "Thanks be to God through Jesus Christ our Lord!" (Romans 7:25). This is the exact reason why Jesus came to earth in the first place; he came to release us from our bondage to sin. "But thanks be to God, that you who were once slaves to sin have become obedient from the heart...having been set free from sin, [and] have become slaves of righteousness" (Romans 6:17–18).

We can't do it ourselves. We will fall every time if we rely exclusively on our own strength and resources. But thanks be to God for a mighty, powerful Savior who can overcome every obstacle and defeat every enemy. St. Paul goes on to say, "There is therefore now no condemnation for those who are in Christ Jesus. For the law of the Spirit of life in Christ Jesus has set me free from the law of sin and death" (Romans 8:1–2). Christ has the power to overcome every addiction, heal every wound, purify every thought, and restrain every evil impulse. The answer to our dilemma—our weapon in this fight—is Jesus himself.

Although sin does remain a challenge even after baptism, it does not have the upper hand. If we entrust ourselves completely to the grace of Christ, we can resist the forces of evil.

> Let not sin therefore reign in your mortal bodies, to make you obey their passions. Do not yield your members to sin as instruments of wickedness, but yield yourselves to God as men who have been brought from death to life, and your members to God as instruments of righteousness. For sin will have no dominion over you, since you are not under the law but under grace. (Romans 6:12–14)

Grace is the key. The life of Christ imparted to us through the sacraments is the answer. Sin will beat us every time if we fight alone; but if we cling to Christ and rely on his saving grace and power, sin will not be able to destroy us.

The grace of Christ is our greatest weapon in the fight against sin. Grace and grave sin are like oil and water. They can't coexist. They are completely incompatible. And the surest way to expel sin is to fill up on grace through the sacraments. This is the reason why we confess any mortal sins before we receive Jesus in the Eucharist. We want our souls to be filled with the fullness of grace so that we can fully receive the King of Grace, Jesus.

Run to Christ. Receive his grace. And sin shall be defeated.

MEETING CHRIST IN OUR TIMES OF NEED

But this raises other questions: How do we run to Christ when we're tempted? Where do we meet him? How do we find him in our times of need?

These are good questions. Our Lord isn't in just one place. Jesus is not restricted to geographical locations. If we are sitting in a coffee shop in Pittsburgh, we can't simultaneously be sitting in an LA movie theater. The reason for this is simple: Our bodies are limited to one place at one time. God, on the other hand, has no such limitations. He is in the Pittsburgh coffee shop and in the LA movie theater—and in every other single place—at the same time with no problem whatsoever. He's God. He's what is known as *omnipresent* (simultaneously in all places). There is no location that escapes his gaze or his presence (see Jeremiah 23:23–24; Acts 17:28). He knows all, sees all, and is in all places.

This is a source of great comfort. Whenever we face temptations and difficulties, all we need to do is call on his name (sometimes out loud) and run to our Savior in prayer and worship. Jesus knows how challenging this life can be—he lived it (though without sin)! The Bible tells us that "we have not a high priest [Jesus] who is unable to sympathize with our weaknesses, but one who in every respect has been tempted as we are, yet without sin" (Hebrews 4:15).

When the Son of God became man, he experienced every challenge that we face (except that he didn't sin). And because of this we are compelled "with confidence [to] draw near to the throne of grace, that we may receive mercy and find grace to help in time of need" (Hebrews 4:16). This remarkable Scripture passage doesn't beat around the bush. With great clarity it reminds us that

Jesus himself underwent temptations. He knows what it's like to undergo such trials. He doesn't have to imagine how hard it is; he knows. He was like us in all ways but sin. Even though he did not suffer the temptations of concupiscence, he knows our condition.

However, unlike us, Jesus remained firm in his commitment to truth and love throughout his life (and death). He was sinless from beginning to eternity. This is good news for us. We have a Lord who understands how powerful temptation can be and yet is even more powerful than the greatest of temptations. Because of this we need to rely on him for help and assistance. We must draw near to him, to his "throne of grace," so that we can receive "help in [our] time of need" (Hebrews 4:16).

The three primary ways we draw close to Christ are through the *sacraments* (especially the Eucharist and confession), *prayer,* and *reading the Bible.* We have to remember this simple yet essential point: *We can't do it on our own; we need Jesus to help us resist temptation and free us from the power of sin.* St. Paul is adamant about the fact that only Christ can give us the "glorious liberty of the children of God" (Romans 8:21). We need Jesus every second of every day. Whenever we feel *even the slightest urge* to look at pornography, go to the party, or accept the bottle, we need to *flee* the scene, *get down* on our knees, and *call out* to our Savior, asking him to give us the strength and power that only he can give.

And if we fall, we need to run to the healing power of Christ found in the sacrament of confession. After discussing the presence of temptation and concupiscence in the Christian life (see CCC 978), the *Catechism* immediately shifts to discussions of confession (979–987). Confession is one of our strongest weapons in the fight against sin. It is one of the greatest gifts Christ gave to his Church (see CCC 981).

> There is no offense, however serious, that the Church cannot forgive.... Christ who died for all men desires that in His Church the gates of forgiveness should always be open to anyone who turns away from sin. (CCC 982)

This is one of the most comforting paragraphs in the whole *Catechism*. Its point is clear: *Jesus is bigger than sin.* There is nothing we could ever do that Christ is unable to heal and forgive. He reigns supreme; he is sovereign. May we never leave his loving, empowering, and all-protecting side, and may we never doubt his ability to restore us to grace when we fall.

What About the "Unforgivable Sin"?

The Bible does talk about an unforgivable sin—in fact, we learn about it from Jesus himself.

> And every one who speaks a word against the Son of man will be forgiven; but he who blasphemes against the Holy Spirit will not be forgiven. (Luke 12:10)

This can be a confusing passage, and there are some people who believe that they have somehow committed this unforgivable sin. More often than not, however, these people are just confused about what exactly blasphemy against the Holy Spirit really is.

The *Catechism* offers some clarity on this troubling issue. It says that "there are no limits to the mercy of God, but anyone who deliberately refuses to accept his mercy by repenting, rejects the forgiveness of his sins and the salvation offered by the Holy Spirit. Such hardness of heart can lead to final impenitence and eternal loss" (CCC 1864). The unforgivable sin is the final refusal to repent of our sins and receive God's forgiveness. We cannot commit the unforgivable sin through a word or statement. We only commit the unforgivable sin when we actively and definitively refuse the offer of God's grace and mercy until death.

The late, great John Paul II hammered this point home by saying: "'Blasphemy' does not properly consist in offending against the Holy Spirit in words; it consists rather *in the refusal to accept the salvation which God offers to man through the Holy Spirit*, working through the power of the Cross." Jesus is constantly offering his love and mercy to us through the Holy Spirit, and "the blasphemy against the Holy Spirit consists precisely in the radical refusal to accept this forgiveness."[13]

In short, the only unforgivable sin is deliberately and finally rejecting God's forgiveness. He does not force his grace and mercy on anyone. It has to be freely embraced. And any person who sincerely asks for mercy will be forgiven.

Thus, if you're worried that you've committed the unforgivable sin, don't be. You haven't. If you *had* committed the unforgivable sin, you wouldn't be worried about it in the slightest. The very fact that you are concerned about the eternal state of your soul and want to receive mercy and forgiveness is proof that you haven't committed blasphemy against the Holy Spirit. Remember: Our God is a God of infinite mercy. He is a heavenly Father who will never withhold his mercy from a repentant person. If you sincerely ask for mercy and seek forgiveness, *you will get it.*

St. Paul experienced God's boundless mercy firsthand. Remember, prior to his conversion, St. Paul was one of the most dangerous men of his time: He killed Christians. The Bible tells us he breathed "threats and murder against the disciples of the Lord" (Acts 9:1). Devoted to the persecutions of Christ's followers, Paul gave active consent to the brutal stoning of St. Stephen (see Acts 7:54—8:1).

As unspeakable as his sins were, however, God was able to forgive Paul and restore him to grace and truth. And not only was he able to forgive St. Paul, God turned him into one of the most important saints in the history of the Church. In spite of his past evils acts, God said that St. Paul would be "a chosen instrument of mine to carry my name before the Gentiles and kings and sons of Israel" (Acts 9:15). St. Paul's life witnesses to the fact that no sin is too great for God to forgive and no person too far gone for God to heal and transform.

How Do I Know for Sure?
I once had a very memorable conversation with an old woman at a Catholic conference. She came up to me after one of my talks and introduced herself by saying that she was a regular at daily Mass, prayed the Rosary, and went to confession on a regular basis. And before I could get a word in edgewise, the woman went on to say something that caught me off guard.

"You know the thing about you I covet the most?" she asked.

I shook my head. She leaned in, lowered her voice to a whisper, and said, "I wish I had your certainty. I go to Mass and pray all the time, but deep down I still wonder whether all of this religious stuff is really as true and powerful as everyone says it is. I wish I had your faith and certainty."

And with that she disappeared into the crowd.

I share this story because I don't think this kindly old woman is unique—I think she's just unusually honest. A lot of us struggle with doubts about what we believe. Many of us accepted the Catholic faith when we were young. We didn't know any better.

We blindly believed whatever our dad or mom or CCD teacher told us.

However, as you grow older and begin to experience the world for yourself, questions and doubts begin to arise. You start to think for yourself. You are less quick to take other people's word for things. You want evidence and proof to validate the claims people make. You look around the world and see a lot of pain and suffering, and somehow this doesn't seem to square with the Christian notion of a good and powerful God. Mass is painfully boring and you wonder if it has any real meaning at all—*they say Jesus is in the Eucharist, but I don't see him...the host just looks like a piece of circular cardboard to me.* These and a myriad of other questions begin to arise about the truth and reality of our faith. And then, like the old woman, the doubts begin to grow within you.

Without a Doubt

This is not uncommon or unusual. Every one of us asks, "How do I know if all of this Christian stuff is true?" at least once in our lives. So if you've ever struggled with doubts about the faith, take comfort in the fact that you're not alone. Some of Jesus's closest friends doubted him as well. We all know that story of doubting Thomas, who refused to believe that Jesus had really resurrected from the dead until he saw the risen Lord with his own eyes and placed his fingers and hands in Christ's wounds (see John 20:24–29). Furthermore, the Gospel writers were honest about the fact that, while most fell down and worshiped Jesus when they saw him after his resurrection, "some doubted" (Matthew 28:17).

Doubt about Christ and the faith is nothing new; it was present from the beginning. And while it is certainly not something to be desired, it is also not fatal to Christ or his Church. Jesus is bigger than our sins, struggles and doubts. He can take whatever challenges befall us and transform them into something glorious. Countless saints wrote and shared of their own personal struggles with doubt. Mother Teresa of Calcutta's own writings to her spiritual director (recorded in the book *Come, Be My Light*) reveal that the tiny saint with the huge heart often struggled with doubt and, even, went years at a time without feeling the love of God.

Doubt is something we all face from time to time. And whenever doubt creeps up on us, we need to remember two main things: First, it isn't the end of the world. Jesus didn't smite Thomas with a bolt of lightning for doubting, and he won't smite us either. Quite the contrary, our Lord went on to make doubting Thomas a great saint and used him to proclaim the Gospel to great multitudes.

Secondly, we need to remember that faith is a gift. We don't create it ourselves. If I am experiencing doubts about the sacred mysteries, no amount of grunting and straining is going to generate faith within me. I can't force myself to believe. The Bible is very clear that faith is something we receive...not create. When St. Peter made the earth-shattering announcement that Jesus was the Christ, the Son of the living God, our Lord noted, "Flesh and blood has not revealed this to you, but my Father who is in heaven" (Matthew 16:17). Peter didn't get his faith by solving a divine equation; his faith was a free gift from God. The *Catechism* also states that "before this faith can be exercised, man must have the grace of God to move and assist him; he must have the interior helps of the Holy Spirit, who moves the heart and converts it to God, who opens the eyes of the mind and 'makes it easy for all to accept and believe the truth'" (CCC 153).

Because faith is a gift, we must run to God whenever we experience doubt. We must be like the man who told Jesus, "I believe; help my unbelief" (Mark 9:24). God wants to give us the gift of faith. He wants us to be able see the beauty of his divine truth and love. Thus, whenever you struggle with doubts, get down on your knees and ask him to remove any obstacles that prevent you from believing. Ask him to open your eyes to the fullness of truth. Ask him to give you the gift of faith...and rest assured that if you are sincere in your search and genuine in your request, God will certainly give you the eyes of faith.

Furthermore, it is important to remember that God is never bothered or offended by our questions. He wants us to learn more. He wants us to seek answers. A young child learns by asking his parents questions like How? and Why? and we as God's children learn by asking the same questions of our heavenly Father. As long as we strive to find truth by trusting in the source of truth—God himself—we will be blessed immensely.

The challenge we face, however, is that some of the things that are most real and true are beyond our finite powers of understanding. And thus we must trust our Lord and Savior to guide us to those truths that are so grand we can't discern them on our own.

(Not) Surprised by Suffering

True happiness is only found in the love of Christ. The Lord is the source of lasting joy and solace. Jesus is the way, the truth, and the life (see John 14:6). There is no real satisfaction and fulfillment apart from him. However, our faith does *not* teach that the challenges of life magically disappear when we enter into a living relationship with Jesus. Christianity is hardly a ticket to heath and wealth, but it is certainly a means to real truth and true love.

Some people think that becoming a follower of Christ will solve all our human problems. From every direction—television, Internet, radio—we are inundated with promises that this or that particular product is the ultimate solution.

Take this pill, and you will lose weight and be beautiful.

Purchase this product, and your every need will be met.

Read this book, and you will never have to study again.

The world is a never ending factory of quick fixes for health, wealth, entertainment, and friends. Why should faith and religion be any different? We've got drive-through restaurants, one-click ordering, and overnight shipping. Shouldn't our faith offer instant gratification, too?

Although it would be nice, this isn't the faith Christ gave us. Sadly, a lot of people come to our Savior expecting him to be the magical element that will give us health, wealth, and earthly success. We expect God to be like a celestial Santa Claus who will give us all of the things we want. "Jesus will make me beautiful, popular and rich, right?" Not necessarily. A life devoted to Christ is not a life of ease and comfort. The Christian life is hard. And the reason for this is simple: Jesus doesn't want to give us only earthly comfort and human success; he wants to give us something infinitely greater: *divine life and heavenly glory.* He wants us to be so united to him that every part of our life and being is transformed by his life and grace. This is awesome, but it's not easy. If we truly follow Christ, we will experience pain and suffering from time to time.

As we've already seen, the sacrament of baptism is the beginning of our life as God's children.

Do you not know that all of us who have been baptized into Christ Jesus were baptized into his death? We were buried therefore with him by baptism into death, so that as Christ was raised from the dead by the glory of the Father, we too might walk in newness of life. (Romans 6:3–4)

In baptism we receive the fullness of grace. Yet, this life is not of some generic variety; it is nothing less than the life of Christ himself. He doesn't give us some life; he gives us his life. Through baptism, we are incorporated into Christ and participate in his sonship. As creatures we live, move, and have our being in him (see Acts 17:28). As our sovereign Lord, he lives, moves, and extends his being in us.

This is the power of Christ's love. It makes us divine children. He unites us to himself and transforms *what* we are into *who* he is. "Baptism not only purifies from all sins, but also makes the neophyte a 'new creature,' an adopted son of God, who has become a 'partaker of the divine nature,' a member of Christ and co-heir with him, and a temple of the Holy Spirit" (CCC 1265). This is the Gospel. This is the grace we have been given. This is the life we are called to live. *We are sons and daughters of God.*

All who are led by the Spirit of God are sons of God.... You have received the spirit of sonship. When we cry, "Abba! Father!" it is the Spirit himself bearing witness with our spirit that we are children of God, and if children, then heirs, heirs of God and fellow heirs with Christ, *provided we suffer with him in order that we may also be glorified with him.* (Romans 8:14–17, emphasis added)

I had always loved Romans 8—at least up until that last verse. This passage confused me. Most of us tend to regard suffering as an indicator of divine displeasure. Suffering is something we expect when we have somehow offended the Almighty. It implies distance between us and our heavenly Father. And yet St. Paul seems to be saying the exact opposite. Not only does he say that it is okay to suffer; he seems to suggest that suffering with Christ is actually a *condition* for our glorification with Christ. *St. Paul says that suffering is something that we, as followers of Jesus, will— not might—experience.*

The apostle goes on to ask: "Who shall separate us from the love of Christ? Shall tribulation, or distress, or persecution, or famine, or nakedness, or peril, or sword (Romans 8:35)?" While most of us would tend to respond with an emphatic "Yes!" St. Paul does not. In fact, he suggests that suffering is one of the things that *unites* us even more fully to the person and work of our Lord. He states that far from separating us from the love of God, "in all these things we are more than conquerors through him [Jesus] who loved us" (Romans 8:37). Suffering is not a sign of defeat. In it we find our victory. Often, it is in the pain that we can encounter Jesus. This is why St. James instructed us to "count it all joy, my brethren, when you meet various trials, for you know that the testing of your faith produces steadfastness...that you may be perfect and complete, lacking in nothing" (James 1:2–4).

The world is a confusing place. Natural disasters, violence, physical ailments, and tragedies seem to plague our every step. While we strive to trust in God's loving care and concern, there are moments in each of our lives when we want to stop, look up to heaven, raise our fist, and ask: "How can you—the all-powerful, sovereign God—permit these things to happen? They say you're a God of love; where is the love in all of this?" Where is God when a gunman opens fire on an elementary school campus, or bombers attack a goodwill-filled sporting event like the Boston Marathon, or when a nation is ravaged by earthquakes or typhoons?

Although it is normal to raise such questions, we must remember that they are often without a human answer. "As the heavens are higher than the earth, so are my ways higher than your ways and my thoughts higher than your thoughts" (Isaiah 55:9). St. Paul understands our confusion, and he sympathizes with our struggles. However, he assures us that "in everything God works for good with those who love him, who are called according to his purpose" (Romans 8:28). Remember: God is sovereign; he is in control. We may not know the particular reasons why God permits certain calamities to arise, but we do know that his loving care and concern remains constant throughout.

God sees more than we see. He loves more than we love. And he is working to bring about a greater good than we could have ever imagined (or accomplished) on our own.

Living His Life, Carrying His Cross

Everyone suffers—even saints and apostles. And while we don't always understand the meaning or purpose behind suffering, St. Paul tells us how we ought to respond when suffering hits.

> I rejoice in my sufferings for your sake, and in my flesh I complete what is lacking in Christ's afflictions for the sake of his body, that is, the church. (Colossians 1:24)

Wow! This verse almost sounds crazy! Not only does St. Paul say that he rejoices in his suffering (something that is utterly bizarre—why would anyone *rejoice* in suffering?), but the apostle also states that he makes up for what is "lacking" in the afflictions of

Christ. How can Christ lack anything? He's God, after all—isn't God's love infinite?

Jesus's love is indeed infinite. In and of itself it lacks nothing. The lack is not located in Jesus; it is located in us. Through our baptism we enter into the life of Christ—*every* part of it, suffering included. Jesus didn't suffer and die so that we don't have to. He suffered and died so that *our* suffering and death (which we can't escape) could be a means to his life.

Suffering is difficult. No one enjoys it. But following Christ means carrying his cross. And the cross is the ultimate sign of this truth and love. St. Josemaría Escrivá said it well:

> You ask me if I had a Cross to bear. And I answered: 'Yes, we always have to bear the Cross.' But it is a glorious Cross, a divine seal, the authentic guarantee of being children of God. That is why, with the Cross, we always travel happily on our way.[14]

We are not alone in the many struggles we face in life. Christ was "made like his brethren in every respect," and since he "has suffered and been tempted, he is able to help those who are tempted" (Hebrews 2:17–18). When you're chained in darkness by the fetters of addiction, you don't call out to a concept but, rather, to a conquerer. When you're kneeling in the cold chapel of a hospital pleading with God to heal your loved one, it's important to feel like he not only hears you but also cares. When the bank is calling daily or when your job and home are all but lost, you look not to a philosophy but to the eternal Philosopher. When you stare at an ultrasound screen that reveals your baby's heart has stopped beating in utero, you aren't just looking for a God who is an idea—you're seeking a consoler and redeemer.

Everyone has a cross to bear, but we must remember we do not bear it alone. We have a loving Savior who can identify with our struggles. He knows the trials we face. We are not alone. "For as we share abundantly in Christ's sufferings, so through Christ we share abundantly in comfort too" (2 Corinthians 1:5). Our Lord loves us. And he will never leave nor forsake us—"he comforts us in all our affliction" (2 Corinthians 1:4).

Our faith is a faith of power and love. It enables us to face all of the struggles of life with and in the life of Christ himself. Trials are real. Difficulties abound. But the grace of our Lord is even more real and even more present.

Jesus loved so that we could love. Jesus gave himself so that we could receive him. He stoops to our level so that we might be raised to his. He is with us in our tears so that we can be with him in his joys. This is his love. This is our faith.

Christ will see us through the hard times. And he won't let go until he has fully situated us with him in the glory of heaven.

You Call This Good News?

We've covered a lot of spiritually explosive ground in this chapter, and I'm sure some of you might be a little freaked out by some of the things we have been discovering in the writings of St. Paul. You may be thinking to yourself, *I thought this book was going to help me feel good about things, but right now I'm just overwhelmed by all this talk about sin, temptation, and suffering.* Some of you may even be discouraged, thinking, *This Christian stuff is harder than I expected… maybe it's harder than it's worth.*

We understand your feelings. But let's clarify a few things. First, Christianity isn't a walk-in-the-park religion—it's a *radical faith.* One of the great tragedies of our modern culture is that so many of us have forgotten just how radical a lifestyle Christianity demands of its followers. Pope Benedict XVI made this point very clear as well. In his first papal encyclical, *Deus Caritas Est* (God Is Love), he said that we're called to embrace a life of love "in its most radical form." By contemplating the radical love of Jesus on the Cross "the Christian discovers the path along which his life and love must move."[15]

This lifestyle of radical love is something we may have forgotten, but fortunately this is something that St. Paul never forgot.

Our faith has to be at the center of everything we do. It has to be at the very center of *who we are*. Love for Jesus Christ needs to be the motivation for our every thought, word, and deed. This "Christ-centeredness" was so important to St. Paul that he decided "to know nothing among you except Jesus Christ and him crucified" (1 Corinthians 2:2). He held nothing back, giving everything to Jesus and his Church: "I do not account my life of any value nor as precious to myself, if only I may accomplish my course and the ministry which I received from the Lord Jesus, to testify to the gospel of the grace of God" (Acts 20:24).

This may sound crazy to some of us, but it made perfect sense to St. Paul because nothing else carries ultimate significance except the person and work of Jesus on the cross (see Galatians 6:14). "For to me to live is Christ, to die is gain" (Philippians 1: 21)." St. Paul treasured his relationship with Jesus above everything and said that he "count[ed] everything as loss because of the surpassing worth of knowing Christ Jesus my Lord" (Philippians 3:8). Paul showed us what it means to rely completely on God in times of difficulty (see 2 Corinthians 1:8–9), and he reminded us that nothing can compare with the joy and happiness awaiting us in heaven (see 2 Corinthians 4:16–17).

The point in all of this is simple: Christ is worth everything! And he wants to free us from this culture of sin and death and lead us to the glories of his heavenly kingdom. It's not an easy journey. Being a child of God can be hard at times, but we shouldn't get discouraged. Discouragement and despair are two of Satan's greatest weapons. The devil knows how powerful Christ is. He knows how beautiful a plan God has for your life. And the last thing the devil wants is for you to find your strength in Christ. His greatest nightmare is your joy in Jesus.

Thus, Satan will do everything in his power to discourage you from following Christ. He will remind you of all your sins, weaknesses, and shortcomings. He will try to get you to believe that you are just too far gone for God to save. Whenever you have these thoughts and feelings, immediately get down on your knees in prayer and remind yourself that there is *no* sin that God can't forgive, no person God doesn't love with a burning passion. Don't let shame and guilt keep you from Christ. Jesus can overcome everything and use anything to bring about his glory. In fact, it is often in our weaknesses that we encounter God's strength (see 2 Corinthians 12:8–10).

Be Not Afraid!

Another tactic that Satan employs in the battle for souls is *fear*. Fear is a subtle thing, and it can take various forms. A lot of us are afraid to face our sinful pasts and admit that we are sinners in desperate need of a savior. We run from ourselves and do everything we can to drown out the truth about who we are and what we've done. I am convinced that this kind of fear is one of the main reasons addictions are so prevalent in our contemporary culture. We are terrified to face our true selves, and we try to lose ourselves in drugs, alcohol, sex, pornography, television, and the Internet—anything to take our minds off of our miserable reality. This is tragic. We need not be afraid. God is sovereign. He knows everything—from the worst thing you've ever done to the greatest thing you'll ever do. There are no surprises to our heavenly Father. He won't run from us, and neither should we run away from our true selves. Instead, we should turn to Jesus, admit our shortcomings and failures, and ask him to do the thing he desires most: heal us from our wounds and transform us by his grace. There is nothing—no sin, evil, or crime—that God can't overcome; there is no wound that he can't heal; there is no person he will turn away. God is love. And he loves you more than you could ever know.

One of the reasons people hesitate to give themselves completely to Jesus is that they are afraid of change. We are creatures of comfort and routine. We have pretty nice lives. Granted, things could be a little better, and we see the advantages to following Christ, but we'd much rather stay put than make any modifications to our world.

This type of fear is unfounded as well. There are times when radical change is necessary. We need to reject anything that prevents us from embracing the fullness of Christ's love. Sometimes that means making some pretty drastic modifications to our lifestyles. For some of us that might mean burning those hidden magazines, getting an Internet filter, chucking those DVDs and CDs, or finding a new group of friends to hang out with. None of these things are easy, but there are times when we need to make some radical changes so that our life can be more centered on Christ and open to his grace.

I SURRENDER ALL

To most of us, the word *surrender* carries a negative connotation. We associate it with defeat. Surrendering is something you do when you have no other options—when you lose. In the world's eyes, surrendering is a sign of weakness.

Not so for the Christian. In fact, far from being a sign of loss or defeat, surrendering is the way we arrive at sure victory and success. When I surrender to God's sovereign plan for my life, he is able to bless me in ways that I couldn't even begin to imagine. All of us are afraid to trust in God. We're afraid he won't know how to make us truly happy. We would much rather make our own plans and decisions and leave God out of it.

Ironic as it is, however, we will only find true happiness if we submit to the plan of God. We will only have victory if we surrender to his loving guidance. St. Paul was adamant about this point: "We know that in everything God works for good with those who love him, who are called according to his purpose" (Romans 8:28). Every part of God's plan is designed for our lasting joy and happiness. He wants you to be happy more than you want to be happy. He wants you to find joy more than you want to find joy. And he is able to give you a delight and pleasure the likes of which no human mind has ever envisioned.

God is a sovereign Father. He is almighty over all, but his power is rooted in his fatherly love. We need to love him completely, give ourselves totally to him, and entrust all that we have to the care of his perfect, loving plan.

God has a plan for your life. Surrender your life to him, and you will find your eternal victory.

FIND YOURSELF IN CHRIST

Surrendering your life to Jesus can be a challenge. Some of us aren't sure who we really are and why we're here. We are all searching for the meaning of life; we are all trying to figure out our purpose, our worth, our identity. Each year dozens of self-help books are written promising their readers answers and tips and tricks on how to wade through life and discover the answers we all seek.

Whether we realize it or not, Jesus Christ is the answer to all of our questions. His love is the only thing that can get us through the hard times. His healing touch is the only thing that can restore us when we fall. His mercy is the only thing that can pull us out of sin and despair. And his grace is the only thing that can provide the eternal happiness we so desperately seek.

I'd be lying if I said that the Christian life is easy. It's not. It's the hardest thing we'll ever have to face. However, the Christian life is also the only thing that can give joy to the sad, strength to the weak, healing to the wounded, and victory to the defeated. God loved us so much that he sent his only Son into the world so that we might be liberated from slavery to sin and given the joys of heaven (see Romans 6:17–23). This is the Gospel. This is our strength. This is our faith. And may we join St. Paul in living every day in the life and love of our beautiful Savior: "For me to live is Christ, and to die is gain" (Philippians 1:21).

::: CHAPTER FIVE :::

. . .

Make Space for Christ
How Man Relates to Others

I received a letter the other day. No, not an e-mail—a letter. When I opened my mailbox, an actual mailbox, and retrieved the envelope (yes, an actual paper envelope, sealed and stamped), it hit me that I hadn't received a letter in years. I receive bills and ads, magazines and Christmas cards. I receive plenty of correspondence from people asking me for money, but a letter—this hadn't happened in quite some time.

I actually got excited. I ripped it open and found several handwritten pages.

Much to my dismay, I came to a disappointing conclusion as I began reading it. I had no idea who the person was who had written the letter. The handwriting was unfamiliar, the greeting was odd, and the story on the opening page mentioned people and situations I knew nothing about.

I turned over the envelope and quickly realized that the letter was not addressed to me. Apparently, our postal worker wasn't used to handling letters very much either because he put someone else's letter in our box. All at once, my balloon of joy popped. I now had to carefully refold and surgically retape the envelope, writing a letter of apology on it to its rightful owner to make up for my overzealous though unintentional felony of opening his mail.

It did strike me, though, just how media-driven and technologically inundated I had become. I couldn't even recall the last time I had received a paper letter; I hadn't felt that feeling of joy in receiving a letter in years. The more I thought about it, most of my communication had been replaced by the phone several years ago…then email…and now text messaging.

In fact, if someone were to ask, "How do you relate to others?" the most popular answer nowadays would probably be Facebook or Twitter.

Can you imagine what far-reaching, global evangelization St. Paul could have done with the Internet? St. Paul would have liked the Internet, seeing in it an inexhaustible tool for spreading the Gospel. What would quickly reveal itself to him, however, is how this tool for potential good can so quickly and easily be manipulated for evil, as well (see Romans 7:21).

This apostle, this saint, constantly challenged the culture of the day, urging man to die to self and sacrifice personally for the good of the Church. He would have liked the intention behind social networking and virtual communities like Facebook, but he also would have seen their potential to become an obstacle to true Christian community. Now, before any Facebook lovers reading this get offended, it's important to make two things clear. First of all, Internet communities like Facebook are not intrinsically evil; like anything on earth, they can be used for good or evil. The choice is in the hands (and hearts) of those posting and reading.

That being said, it's vital for anyone in today's online communities to answer the following questions: "Are my actions, words, pictures, and profiles glorifying God, my Savior? Does my page or my postings reflect a focus on God or on myself? Am I an arrow pointing *others* to God or to myself?" If the answers to these questions are not God-focused, then the odds are you're wasting an incredible opportunity to share his love with others.

This chapter is about how people (you and me and everyone) relate to each other.

The point is not to condemn Facebook; it is just one example of a much larger struggle we have as the children of God—the struggle for authenticity and true community.

Two Versions of Self

How many people know the *real* you? Not the you that you portray to the world, but the true, authentic you, in all of your brattiness, moodiness, selfishness, ego, and pride?

What a fun way to begin a chapter, right? We have to start here, though, if we really want to understand where St. Paul wants to lead us. Even if you don't utilize Twitter or Facebook, the truths and themes we're discussing here are easily transferable to any and all relationships you currently have, so keep reading.

Remember back in chapter three when we talked about self-awareness? It's important to recognize that self-awareness isn't just awareness of oneself but also an awareness of how others view that self. Online communities like Facebook are engaging and dynamic—and also very telling. Peoples' profiles usually demonstrate two distinctly different things: How people *want* to be seen and, as a result, how people *are actually* seen.

We often have two versions of ourselves. The first version is the person seen by most of the world, the person we try to portray in our conversation, dress, attitudes, and personality (like on our Facebook pages). People use backgrounds, videos, text, and pictures to communicate things about themselves to all who visit their page(s). Biographies tell the world what we want them to know about us—everything from our current mood to our latest thoughts and favorite books (that we haven't finished), to what television and films are currently forming our daily morality. Many of us proudly portray images of ourselves on Facebook, for instance, that we want others to consider authentic displays of our innermost beings. Version one is a usually more of a self-portrait.

The second version is the one that comes out in real life, usually only around those you love and live with. The second version is the real you, the one that rears its early morning bedhead for only a select few to see. It's the version of you when the makeup is off, the pajamas are on, the hair isn't combed, and you're surrounded only by those who are legally obligated to love you. Would the people who see *this* version of you say that your Facebook profile is an accurate assessment of who you are? An even deeper question would be, "Would *God* look at your Facebook profile and rejoice, because it represented all he hopes for you to be?" Beyond Facebook, would God look at your relationships at school, work and home, and thank you for putting his truth and his will ahead of your wants? Do you relate to others with a godly perspective?

Modern media gurus say that handheld devices and the Internet have revolutionized the way we communicate with and relate to one another. St. Paul would offer a different answer. Technology is fine, he would say, but when asked how man relates to others, Paul would offer just a one-word answer: love.

If you say, "That's a nice idea, but that's not how it is," you could have lived in Rome a couple of thousand years ago. It was to hardened hearts like ours that St. Paul wrote. For Paul, truly loving one another was not some fairy-tale fantasy. It was achievable, but with a catch: It had to start with you, not someone else. It's easy to say, "I love you" with your words, but true love isn't about words, it's about actions.

Jesus showed us—and Paul reminds us—that our actions will always, ultimately, be motivated by the absence or presence of one thing: love.

True Love Is the Answer

Have you ever seen the crucifixion of your Savior? Not in a movie, but in your own heart, during prayer? Have you ever truly pictured Golgotha, where Christ was sacrificed for you?

Try to picture it now. When the earthquake subsided and the darkness lifted that Friday afternoon, it must have resembled something like a crime scene. Ask the Holy Spirit to guide your mind and heart now as you envision the site.

Survey the rocky ground. Feel the stones crushing one another and moving beneath your feet. Hear the eerie wind whistle through the valley below, muffling the sobbing of your Mother, Mary. See the bloodstained rocks and cloths that surround the site. Notice the indifference of the guards on duty. Hear the mockery and gossip of the remaining onlookers. Ask yourself why anyone would perform such an unspeakable act upon another human being, much less allow such an act when he had the power to stop it instantly.

Now, look forward to where the wood enters the stony ground. Let your eyes slowly track up the blood-stained wood. See the spike driven through his feet. Witness the flesh hanging from his bones like ribbons. Look at the nails in his hands, the hands that washed feet and broke bread. Look upon your Savior, again, as though for the very first time.

On Good Friday, love conquered the great divide between God and man and between God's children.

Man relates to others, to one another, in the same way in which God relates to man...through love. Mankind comes together in times of suffering but, ultimately, what brings people together, even more than mutual suffering, is sacrificial love. Love conquers the greatest divides of hatred, racism, greed, lust, sexism, etc., but it doesn't stop there—love conquers sin and destroys death. That is how Christ defeated Satan, not merely with the blood of sacrifice, but with the blood, sweat, and tears of love.

How can such a gruesome sight simultaneously be so beautiful? The answer is this: love. It was because of the love involved.

Love Requires Bodily Sacrifice

Love is the answer. I don't mean that figuratively; I mean it literally. To every question asked, the answer is love because, to Paul, love was the answer to every question (see 1 Corinthians 13).

When St. Paul envisioned the cross of Christ, he saw in Jesus what our heavenly Father sees: perfect love. St. Paul must have had the crucifix engrained in his mind and emblazoned on his heart when he penned the following words to the Romans:

> I appeal to you, therefore, brethren, by the mercies of God,
> to present your bodies as a living sacrifice, holy and acceptable to God, which is your spiritual worship. (Romans 12:1)

Offering our bodies as a sacrifice can be looked at in two ways. The first way involves the do nots, as in do not have premarital sex, do not look at pornography, do not use profanity, do not be lustful, and do not abuse your bodies with drugs or alcohol. These are obvious sins, and St. Paul definitely would have included all of them (and many more) in what we ought to sacrifice. True sacrifice like the kind mentioned in this verse, however, goes even deeper into the dos, as well, as in what Christians *should* do with their bodies. We should pray, serve others, work for justice, remain pure, affirm others, live the virtues, etc. This verse is simultaneously telling us to "put to death" the deeds of the flesh (Romans 8:13) and to be righteous (see Romans 6:13).

St. Paul is telling us to be countercultural. Most in the world put themselves first. He is calling us to change our attitudes and free our minds with the Gospel message, to reject worldliness and selfishness.

"Do not be conformed to this world but be transformed by the renewal of your mind, that you may prove what is the will of God, what is good and acceptable and perfect" (Romans 12:2).

St. Paul warns us about people who twist the truth (see Romans 1:18–32; 2 Timothy 4:1–6). Modern wannabe philosophers claim to have truth but offer little more than self. God's will must guide us in all circumstances, otherwise it is "our will be done," which was Adam's sin. Living like Christ, the new Adam, means we seek God's will and *that* is how we are transformed into God's image (see Romans 8:29), how we become "good and acceptable and perfect."

Christ's identity and kingship were not made known by the sign above his head which proclaimed his title. Christ's identity upon that wood was made known by the beautiful and mangled body that hung beneath the placard. Words didn't proclaim the king-ship of Jesus; the sacrifice of his body did. It's not the sign on the parish you attend that makes you a Catholic. It's not the words on the T-shirt, the message on the bumper sticker, the rosary hanging from the rearview mirror, or the title on the parochial uniform that makes you a Catholic.

It's what you do with your body (and what you don't do) that makes you a true Catholic, a true Christian. St. Paul understood this fact and lived it out with the core of his being. We can learn a lot from him.

That is what the body of Christ does—it dies, out of love, in order to rise and bring life. Why did Christ die? The answer is: love.

There Is No I in Team (But There Are Three in Humiliation)

We were humiliated by the loss. Hundreds of hours of training, countless days icing sore joints and heating muscles, and all the eight of us had to show for it was a last-place finish. It was a diffi-cult way to learn an important lesson. I had made our collegiate crew rowing team several months earlier, even though I had never rowed in a boat before, much less rowed competitively. I quickly learned how difficult a sport it was to master.

I had begun training in an eight-man boat with the other novices. Our coach, called a coxswain, was amazed at how a few of us had gelled and adapted so quickly. Not long after, four of us who (apparently) showed promise were moved to our own, smaller shell (boat). We immediately excelled. Our movements were synchronized. We were four bodies functioning as one, and we won, a lot—so much so, that when we were asked to rejoin the eight-man shell for a race, we were convinced that we could turn the other four rowers into champions like ourselves. To quote Scripture, as St. Paul often did, "Pride [went] before destruction" (Proverbs 16:18).

We had grown so comfortable with just our team of four that we didn't bother to adapt to or to include the other quartet in our race. We were favored to win; instead we came in dead last. Twice, our shell stalled, once almost capsizing, because our eight oars were not functioning in unison. The blades were not at the same angles. The strokes were not at the same speeds. Put simply, we were one in name only, but our team was not a true team at all. Had we taken advantage of one another's gifts, talents, and individual skill sets, we assuredly would have won. We failed not because we lost; we failed because of pride. We had the individual talent but not the unity.

One Body, Filled with Gifts

I wish St. Paul could have been the coxswain of our crew team. He would have coached us and guided us with the wisdom of Christ like he offered those in Rome. Do not think of yourself more highly than you ought, Paul would have warned us (see Romans 12:3). You all have gifts that differ, according to God's grace, he would have reminded us (see Romans 12:6).

Our gifts and talents are just that—gifts—that come from God's grace. The Greek word for *grace* is *charis* which is the root word for "gift" (*charismata*). Incidentally, that's why the spiritual gifts of tongues or prophecy or teaching and preaching are considered charismatic gifts. The term *charismatic* doesn't just refer to a movement or a style of prayer; it literally means "gift."

Paul offers a quick overview of some of the spiritual *gifts* in Romans 12:4–8, and a far more in-depth examination of them in 1 Corinthians 12. These verses are worth a prayerful read. Understanding the spiritual gifts and the mystical body of Christ requires more than a pragmatic, logical approach—it necessitates a prayerful discernment of the heart, including discernment of your own spiritual gifts, which you may have yet to really tap into. Spiritual gifts are like muscles: If they're not used, they atrophy. God endows us all with gifts; he gives them freely but he expects us to use them. Like any family, our Father expects us to share.

CHILDREN SHARE, BRATS DON'T

God's hope and, frankly, his expectation is that "as each has received a gift, [we would] employ it for one another, as good stewards of God's varied grace" (1 Peter 4:10). Seeing the link between God's grace and our gifts is vital because Paul wants us to remember that everything comes from God. The only thing in this world that is all ours is our sin. Everything else is a gift from God, our Father.

If Paul had been my coxswain, I could have said to him, "But I really worked hard at crew. I woke up every morning at 4:00 A.M., I ran six miles a day, and I rowed for three hours a day. We didn't just deserve to win because of our God-given athletic ability, but because of our hard work." Paul would have smirked, shaken his disbelieving head, and reminded me that *even my work ethic* is a gift from God. God doesn't give people gifts that he doesn't want them to use for his glory. So, as Paul said, "Let us use them" (Romans 12:6). We should use God's gifts, constantly, for his glory, not our own.

In doing what we ought, we deserve no praise, because it is
our duty.[16] —St. Augustine

As a good coach, though, he wouldn't have stopped there. He
would have wanted to be sure that we understood why we failed
to achieve our goal of victory, why we failed to finish the race
(1 Corinthians 9:24; 2 Timothy 4:7). We functioned singularly;
we focused more on ourselves than each other, and that's not
Christian.

For as in one body we have many members, and all the
members do not have the same function, so we, though
many, are one body in Christ, and individually members one
of another. (Romans 12:4–5)

As sons and daughters in Christ, which we are as we discussed
in chapter two, we belong to one another. Like the old-school
Christmas lights on a strand, if one bulb burns out the rest of the
strand is useless, it cannot achieve its purpose or function. We are
all connected in the mystical body of Christ; we need one another.
In fact, it's God's will that we need one another (CCC 1937).

Christ taught us this principle in the parable of the talents
(Matthew 25). God gives different measures of gifts to different
people so that we will work together and rely upon one another in
love. Our gifts are complimentary; that is to say, they only realize
their full potential when used in conjunction with others' gifts in
Christ.

We form and build this one body when we share not only our
material goods or our personal talents, but when we share our
spiritual gifts, as well. The Church teaches about this when she
speaks of solidarity. Simply put, solidarity can be thought of as

"all for one and one for all...for a specific goal." Far more deeply, the Church tells us that "solidarity is an eminently Christian virtue" (CCC 1948).

What the Church is telling us is that for us to live a truly virtuous life, we must not only have concern for others, we must actively work for one another's salvation (see 1 Peter 1:9). For we, as believers, to become all that God designed us to become, we must see our faith walk as being connected to everyone else's faith walk and then next, *do something about it*. Solidarity is shown through sharing not only our material gifts but also our spiritual gifts and our sacrificing for others.

And *why* do we sacrifice for others? Why do we offer our gifts in service to our brothers and sisters? The answer is: love.

It's Social Justice, not Social Just Us

How would you feel if you worked hard in your job each day, only to have your paycheck withheld from you? You would be upset, to say the least. How about if you had your home taken from you without reason? What would you do if you didn't have enough money to feed yourself or your children? Would you resort to a life of crime? Would you strike back at those who were unjust toward you? What if you desperately needed help from others but were turned away because of your religion or skin color or age? What if you had no voice and no right to speak? What if you were denied your right to worship freely? What if someone in worldly authority decided to rescind your right to live? What if your life wasn't worth much in the eyes and mind and philosophy of another? That would not be justice, and that is not of God.

We receive our human dignity from God; we are created in his image. Man, all mankind, is endowed with *transcendent dignity*.

Transcendent means "coming from beyond our normal, physical human experience." In other words, life doesn't just come from a man and woman having sex, but from the man, the woman, *and God*. *Dignity* means "the inherent and unchanging value of a person, created in God's own image and likeness." Our worth comes not from what we do or what we offer society—our worth comes from the one from whom we came.

We (you and I) are endowed with a worth that is beyond this world, a worth that cannot and should not be destroyed by this world—because all life ultimately came, comes, and will come only from God.

Paul didn't offer these teachings as philosophy like many of his Greek contemporaries did. No, for Paul, justice and solidarity were inseparably linked with true Christian living. Paul didn't look at service or justice as theoretical, but as very practical.

> We, though many, are one body in Christ, and individually
> members of one another. Having gifts that differ according
> to the grace given to us, let us use them. (Romans 12:5–6)

God freely gives us his grace, and so we ought freely to give our gifts and ought to put them at the service of others (see 1 Peter 4:10), especially those most in need. The *Catechism* sums it up beautifully, saying, "The duty of making oneself a neighbor to others and actively serving them becomes even more urgent when it involves the disadvantaged" (CCC 1932). This is what it means when Christ says, "Whatever you do to the least of my brothers, you do to me" (see Matthew 25:40). Take the time to immerse yourself in the Church's wisdom on this subject (see CCC 1928–1948).

It's been said that love is blind; justice is supposed to be blind, as well. Many modern day Christians, including Catholics, often pick and choose the Gospel elements they wish to follow. Some speak out intently and passionately about the immigration debate but remain silent regarding abortion. Others pray rosaries outside abortion clinics but quickly dismiss those of other cultures or ethnicities most in need of humanitarian aid and relief. St. Paul is very intentional in the way he advocates that Christians look out for one another and serve one another in mutual affection. He reminded the folks in Ephesus that "the work of ministry [is] building up the body of Christ" (Ephesians 4:12).

True Christians, as Paul notes, must embrace the entire gospel of life, the gospel our Roman Catholic Church upholds in the face of all obstacles—political, social, and physical.

How can you best love Christ? Seek justice.

How can you best love all of mankind? Seek Christ.

How can you embrace the *entire* Gospel of life? With love.

Communion Isn't Just a Sunday Thing

Solidarity requires communion. Justice requires communion. So now the only question is, "What is communion, exactly?"

When you hear the word *communion*, you probably think of rising from your pew during Mass and walking forward to receive the Eucharist. In truth, though, communion is not just the action of going forward to receive Jesus in his precious Body and Blood; true communion means becoming *one with God*.

The dictionary defines *communion* as "an exchange of intimate thoughts and feelings." And while the good folks at Webster do a nice job, that definition doesn't go nearly deep enough. Communion in Christ is more than sharing common feelings and more than expressing intimate feelings. The Christian life is about learning how to surrender to God; it is a gift of self. True communion (in Christ) is giving yourself back to God *and to* his children It is the Holy Spirit who brings us into communion with Christ. St. Paul tells us that it is only by the Holy Spirit that we can even proclaim that Christ is Lord (1 Corinthians 12:3). The same way Christ leads us into a more intimate relationship with God the Father, the Holy Spirit leads us into a more intimate relationship with Christ.

In addition, we are called to be in communion not only with Christ, but with his body, the Church. The Latin root word for communion, *communio*, means "common"—we are bound together with the greater body of Christ, a body of believers with whom we share *common* beliefs and *common* realities. One of the "realities" we share is that God is God and we are not; God is the creator, and we are his creation.

At Holy Mass we come together, in community (same root word), entering into physical and spiritual communion with one another and with God. At that same time, we are surrounded by all the saints and angels (see Hebrews 12:1), in *communion* with the mystical body of Christ (the *communion* of saints) who have gone before us. In God's timelessness, we are worshipping alongside the heavenly host (saints and angels), during this re-presentation of Christ's once-and-for-all perfect sacrifice, in perfect communion. Then, during the Mass, we receive Communion (Christ's true sacramental presence) in order that we might become saints ourselves.

One Body—Through Him, with Him, in Him

The Holy Mass is a celebration of Christ's sacrifice to the Father. It is taking place every moment of every day (except on Good

Friday) in some corner of the world. Masses have been offered and celebrated on land and sea and in the air. The Mass has taken place on battlefields and in castles, in prisons and in jungles, in stadiums and in catacombs. Thousands of times every Sunday throughout the world, we hear the same readings and the same words of consecration.

Catholics are united and bound by this sacrifice, the one true meal that surpasses time, geography, language, class, and race. At the Eucharistic table of our Lord, we become one body, as we become one with his Body.

The Mass is a liturgy—the Liturgy of the Word and the Liturgy of the Eucharist. Liturgy is a public work, done in the service of another, which means that we don't only go to receive, but also to give. The common misconception is that we go to Mass only to receive Jesus in the Scriptures (Word) and in his flesh and blood (Eucharist). While this is true, it is not the sole purpose of going to Mass. You are at Mass to offer your witness and your love. You are there for the people sitting around you, those experiencing the highs and the lows that come with a life lived for Christ. In offering your body and your presence, you follow the example of Christ, who is truly physically present under the appearance of bread and wine.

> The cup of blessing...is it not a participation in the blood of Christ? The bread which we break, is it not a participation in the body of Christ? Because there is one bread, we who are many are one body, for we all partake of one bread. (1 Corinthians 10:16–17)

St. Paul absolutely believed in Christ's true presence in the Eucharist, which we will go into in more detail later. What is vital to understand, is that for St. Paul, we are not just called to be emotionally united to one another, but personally united as well. At no time is the body of Christ more connected or more one than when we are at the Mass. Of course, that doesn't mean that we won't have conflicts; every family has controversy. We even offer a time in Mass for reconciliation with our brothers and sisters in the body of believers, during the sign of peace. What should this teach us?

How ought we handle controversy within the one body of Christ? That's right...with love.

FAMILY FEUD—DEALING WITH CONTROVERSY
Sometimes people mistakenly believe that to be Christian means never arguing and disagreeing. Nothing could be further from the truth. Our Lord himself warned us to anticipate disagreements. Living as a Christian doesn't mean that we shouldn't ever disagree, but it does mean that we need to learn how to disagree respectfully and argue with love. Ask yourself this question: "When I argue with people, is it out of a desire to get them to hear me or to *get them to heaven?*" If it's not the latter, it's not worth the argument, because it's not of God.

To constantly and consistently love others, even those we disagree with or have a conflict with, is how we "outdo one another in showing honor" as St. Paul directs us to do in Romans 12:10. Listen, again, to his advice to the Christians in Colossae, regarding the need to live in peace and to seek love:

> Put on then, as God's chosen ones, holy and beloved, compassion, kindness, lowliness, meekness, and patience, forbearing one another and, if one has a complaint against another, forgiving each other; as the Lord has forgiven

you, so you must also forgive. And above all these put on love, which binds everything together in perfect harmony. (Colossians 3:12–14)

Did you catch what St. Paul said "binds everything together in perfect harmony"? The answer is love.

Compassion and kindness, meekness, and patience all require love, and love requires living in the truth. Some modern Christians employ, the excuse, "Well, I wouldn't do it, but I'm not going to tell someone else how to live their life." St. Paul would have much stronger words. He'd warn us about casting judgment (see Romans 14), yes, but he'd warn us even more sternly about being so careless about others' sins. In doing so, we show that we care less about their souls.

Not correcting our brothers and sisters who are in sin is a sin of omission, a sin against the body of Christ. Jesus was quite clear when he commanded us: "Take heed to yourselves; if your brother sins, rebuke him, and if he repents, forgive him" (Luke 17:3). In instances such as these, keeping silent is not loving. Speaking difficult truth—the truth of Christ and his Church—*that* is true love.

Speaking the truth in love, we are to grow up in every way into Him who is the head, into Christ, from whom the whole body, joined and knit together by every joint with which it is supplied, when each part is working properly, makes bodily growth and upbuilds itself in love. (Ephesians 4:15–16)

Now, that being said, some people (yes, even Christians) are far too quick and far too willing to point out all their brothers' sins, and the sins of their brothers' brother, his wife, her aunt, her cousin, her co-worker—and anyone else they hear about. Gossip is a sinful and deadly habit. Paul reminds us that we'd be wise to only offer fraternal correction after we've taken a long, hard look at ourselves. It's difficult to find the splinters in someone else's life with a huge beam sticking out of our own eyes (see Matthew 7:3–5).

The motivation of pointing out someone's sin is for that person's salvation and the good of the mystical body, not for embarrassment or to increase your reputation, appearance, or position. True Christian brotherhood and sisterhood requires not only the willingness to point out (in love) someone else's sin, but the willingness to forgive the grievance, no matter how severe, even if it was inflicted upon you.

Fraternal correction is a common theme throughout St. Paul's writings. A closer examination of his work reveals a heart that understands the power of forgiveness, on personal and corporate levels (Romans 4:7–8). The more you pray and read through Paul's writings, the more you'll see *what he saw,* namely that forgiveness requires power and not weakness (see Galatians 6:1–10, Colossians 3:12–13, 2 Corinthians 7:8–9) and that power changes the world in a way that swords never could. Remember, we're supposed to be building one another up (Romans 14:19).

It's been said that to err is human, to forgive, divine. We know that sinning is human, but we sometimes forget that if we really want to be like Christ and live in his divine image, we must forgive.

And how do we forgive when we have been hurt? The answer is: with love.

Do You Want the Good News or the Bad News?
The bad news is that if you follow Christ, you are going to die.

The good news is that Christ beat death, so if follow him, you will live.

The bad news is that following him means *a lot* of personal sacrifice.

The good news is that he gives you the Holy Spirit to help you.

Let's explore each of these four truths briefly, one at a time.

If You Follow Christ, You Are Going to Die.

The Acts of the Apostles is one of the underrated jewels of the New Testament. Often called "the Gospel of the Holy Spirit," Acts bears witness to the explosion of the early Church through the power of the Spirit; it offers valuable insights into the early saints, in particular, Peter and Paul.

The Acts of the Apostles was written by St. Luke, who was also a traveling companion of St. Paul. There is a line in the first chapter of Acts that is often glossed over by the quick read, but (as is the case with most Scripture) a deeper, more prayerful reading of the verse opens up whole new levels of its meaning. We'll pause and reflect on it now, before we move on:

> You shall receive power when the Holy Spirit has come upon
> you; and you shall be my witnesses. (Acts 1:8)

Read this verse again, but this time, instead of saying "witnesses," use the Greek word for witness, which is *martyr*.

What does it take for someone to lay down their life for the Gospel? What does it take to turn Simon Peter, a fisherman, into *the* shepherd? What does it take to turn Saul, a murderer, into a martyr? It takes a personal encounter with the living God, an intimate relationship with Jesus Christ.

If you have a difficult time really connecting with the saints and martyrs, it might be because they don't seem real to you. Possibly their sacrifices seem so great or their lives so noble, that it makes them unreachable. Perhaps the stories read more like fiction than real life. Possibly, faith has never come to life *in your life* in a way that causes you to be willing to sacrifice your life. If that's the case, you're not alone. The pews are filled each week with people who have the desire to love God but who fear total surrender to him to the point of death.

There is one very real dilemma every Christian must come to terms with, however—namely, that Jesus Christ is real and so are these disciples mentioned in Scripture. The Scripture accounts are not fairy tales or legends. Paul walked the earth. Paul was stoned by others. Paul was whipped and flogged. Paul was shipwrecked and beaten and imprisoned (see 2 Corinthians 11:23–29), and ultimately he was beheaded. The Bible contains real stories with real people and real life and death consequences.

This is such a great reality that the Church sets aside a feast day (June 28) just to commemorate the martyrdom of Sts. Peter and Paul. Pope Benedict XVI declared an entire year of St. Paul to commemorate the life and contribution of this heroic saint. Peter and Paul aren't remembered solely for their early Church importance or accomplishments, but for their faithful martyrdom.

Do you see the importance of that proclamation of faith? People don't give their lives for ideas. People don't give their lives for philosophies. People don't even give their lives, necessarily, for wonder workers. People give their lives for truth and for freedom—they give their lives for the love of God.

If we spend more time focusing on what it takes to lay down our lives for *someone* (and not just *something*), we will begin to understand the difference between martyrdom and senseless, historical *homicide*. Soon, we will see the intimacy with Christ required for such an act. Most of you reading this will never be asked to lay down your physical life for the Gospel. You will, however, be challenged several times a day or a week to lay down your life in social situations, in tempting situations, in morally challenging situations; you will be asked to die to yourself and to public opinion, and to live for the truth of the Gospel.

How do you find the love and courage to die for the truth, for the faith, for *the* God?

The answer is: with love.

Now, for the good news...

If You Follow Christ, You Will Live.

Why do you go to Church? Why do you pray? Why do you listen to Christian music or wear a Christian T-shirt? Why do you serve at your parish or raise your family in the faith? Why do you go on retreats or head to reconciliation when others don't?

You might have several different answers to the questions above, but they should all come from the same reason. St. Peter summed it up pretty well when he said, "The goal of our faith is salvation" (see 1 Peter 1:9).

Do you get it? *Salvation* is the reason we do the things we do in our faith. Salvation, yours and others', is the reason you go to Mass. Salvation is why you and I should be willing to be witnesses (martyrs) with Christ for God's truth. We, like the apostles, are commissioned to bring the Gospel to the ends of the earth (see Matthew 28:16–20); commissioned means that we are coworkers (1 Corinthians 3:9) in Christ's mission, offering truth to a world that desperately needs it, offering light to the blind and freedom to souls enslaved in darkness.

Perhaps you have people in your life, family members or friends, whom you desperately want to know the love of God. Have you ever wanted it for them more than they wanted it for themselves? Are there people in your life who look at Jesus as merely a nice guy, with good stuff to say?

Jesus is often seen as a philosopher more than as a Savior; *religion* has become a dirty word for a lot of people. It's unfortunate that in today's world, when so many people are in need of hope, looking for answers, and seeking clarity in their lives, people overlook the one voice that is actually offering freedom and truth: the voice of Christ.

The question you might often hear from someone who is good-hearted but anti-religion is, "What difference does it make, really?" The answer is: all the difference in this *and* the next world. The truth is:

Without God, suffering is pointless.

Without God, our vocations (and our joy) become self-motivated.

Without God, other things like sex, work, money, or relationships become our focus.

Without God, marriage is just a legal agreement.

Without God, there is no heaven; when it's over, it's over; death is final.

But *with Christ*, everything changes.

As St. Paul pointed out:

With Christ, suffering has purpose (Romans 5:3; Ephesians 3:13; 2 Thessalonians 1:5; 2 Timothy 1:8; 2:3–9).

With Christ, our vocations bring freedom
(Romans 8:28, 11:29; Ephesians 1:11, 2:10; Philippians
2:13; 1 Corinthians 1:26).

With Christ, we aren't mastered by the world
(Romans 8:5–13, 13:14; Ephesians 5:3; Colossians 3:5; 1
Timothy 3:3; 2 Timothy 3:2; 1 Corinthians 5:11).

With Christ, marriage is a covenant of service
(Romans 7:2–3; 1 Corinthians 7:2–4; Ephesians 5:23, 33; 2
Corinthians 11:2).

With Christ, death is defeated and life is eternal
(Romans 2:7, 6:10, 22–23, 8:38; 1 Corinthians 15:47–48;
2 Corinthians 4:10–12; Ephesians 1:10, 3:15; Philippians
3:20; Colossians 1:5, 20; 1 Thessalonians 4:16, 5:8).

St. Paul understood that, in Christ, all things come into their proper perspective. Jobs are just that, jobs. Money is something, *not* everything. Marriage is a living example of love, not a dying example of annoyance. Through Christ, the big things don't overtake us, and the little things have significance. With Jesus, you are never alone even when you feel lonely, and you are never without hope even when you're feeling empty; God's love remains (see 1 Corinthians 13:13). That's the *good* news.

Jesus Christ offers us life. He also offers us a greater understanding and vision. With Jesus in your life, you begin to trust that there is a purpose you were created for and a vocation only you can fulfill (see Jeremiah 29:11). God wants to reach those people in your life you're worried about, as well as those you don't even know yet. The way he does that is through the Gospel, and the way he delivers his gospel is through you.

How do you you share the good news, you may ask? The answer is: with love.

Following Him Means Personal Sacrifice.

Is St. Paul's take on the world what you experience at school or at work? Is this the message modeled around your family dinner table? How about on Facebook? Is this the message that you receive or that you spread on Twitter? If not, why not?

Remember, it was what Christ did with his body that demonstrated *who* he was. Are you willing to rise to St. Paul's challenge to offer your body as a living sacrifice (see Romans 12:1)? Will you refuse to conform yourself to this age (see Romans 12:2)?

Does your online profile on Facebook, for instance, need to change to better reflect the light of Christ? If so, change it. Does your demeanor at school or work need to change in order for people to know you take your faith seriously? Does your dress, your attitude, your language, your integrity, your modesty, your personality, or anything else about you need an overhaul for people really to see Christ in you? St. Paul, like a good coach, would tell you to stand up and get going, because there are souls at stake, including your own.

> Let us then cast off the works of darkness and put on the armor of light; let us conduct ourselves becomingly as in the day, not in reveling and drunkenness, not in debauchery and licentiousness, not in quarreling and jealousy. (Romans 13:12–13)

St. Paul wasn't just singling out the Christians in Rome, either. No, Paul knew this would be a struggle for every Christian, us included. He made similar points to the people in Ephesus, Thessalonica, and Galatia.

You might be asking yourself, Why should I sacrifice like this? Why should I change? Because changing is what it *really means* to be a true Christian. Christianity (as we see with Christ on the cross) means dying to yourself and your own comforts so that others might live. It is difficult to do. It won't be easy. It won't be popular most of the time. It never has been.

This is why St. Paul's words to the Romans are so timeless. The early Christians were going through the same struggles that we do. He encouraged them to "put on the Lord Jesus Christ" (Romans 13:14), to clothe themselves in purity. Paul warned them never to put "a stumbling block or hindrance in the way of a brother" (Romans 14:13). And, he reminded us that, "each one of us shall give account of himself to God" (Romans 14:12). We will be held accountable and judged by how we sacrificed for others.

It's not enough to talk about Jesus with people. We need to seek to *become* what God desires. We need to do what Jesus did on the cross and offer our "bodies as a living sacrifice" (Romans 12:1). Living like a Christian means that "if your brother is being injured by what you [do], you are no longer walking in love" (Romans 14:15). It means that we should look for ways to build one another up, not tear each other down (see Romans 14:19). It means that it's not enough to look out for yourself and your own holiness only but remember that you "who are strong ought to bear with the failing of the weak" (Romans 15:1). As "Christ became a servant" (Romans 15:8), we must become servants, too.

How can this become more than just a nice idea? The answer is: with love. How can you make Facebook more like *Hisbook?* That's right! With love.

God Gives You the Holy Spirit to Help You.

Most Catholics don't feel that they are worthy of sainthood. Let's face it, most of you reading this don't really believe that you could become a saint. "That's for people like Mother Teresa or Pope John Paul II," you'd probably say. "I'm not *that* holy." The truth of the matter, however, is that you are called to be a saint. The even greater truth (and better news) is that, with the Holy Spirit, sainthood is actually attainable.

Do you want practical examples of how you become a saint? Let's look at what St. Paul says in Romans 12:9–21, but rather than reading it like a Scripture passage, let's read it like a laundry list. Here are the twenty-five things you should do daily to become a living saint. It's actually pretty simple:

Let [your] love be genuine.

Hate what is evil; hold fast to what is good.

Love one another with brotherly affection.

Outdo one another in showing honor.

Never flag [grow weary] in zeal.

Be aglow [on fire] with the Spirit.

Serve the Lord.

Rejoice in your hope.

Be patient in tribulation.

Be constant in prayer.

Contribute to the needs of the saints.

Practice hospitality.

Bless those who persecute you and do not curse them.

Rejoice with those who rejoice.

Weep with those who weep.

Live in harmony with one another.

Do not be haughty.

Associate with the lowly.

Never be conceited.

Repay no one evil for evil.

Take thought for what is noble in the sight of all.

Live peaceably with all as far as it depends on you.

Never avenge yourselves; leave it to God.

If your enemy is hungry, feed him; if he is thirsty, give him drink.

Do not be overcome by evil, but overcome evil with good.

Notice that, while I said sainthood is *attainable*, I didn't say *it* was easy. All the commands on the above list are practical and active—just like all of St. Paul's advice. While Paul is very philosophical, he's also very practical. He doesn't want us to think that Christianity is all about ideas or emotions (see 1 John 3:18). These commands are rooted in the Gospels and remind us that our attitudes, decisions, *and* our sins affect the entire body of Christ. We cannot be indifferent to one another or blind to our own sins, because we are all one body, united in Christ (see Romans 12:4–5).

Mark this page of the book. Let this list serve as the foundation for your daily life. Soon you'll see why St. Paul refers to the word of God as the "sword of the Spirit" (Ephesians 6:17) and not a sword made of metal, the likes of which took his head and sent him home to heaven.

If this list struck you as very difficult to do on a daily basis, that's good—it shows you're honest with yourself about where you are spiritually; that is self-awareness. Offering your body as "a living sacrifice" (Romans 12:1) isn't easy. The sacrifice of *one glorious body* upon a cross shows everybody how to live and act as one body, in love...that we might live "no longer for ourselves, but for God" (2 Corinthians 5:15). That is how *MySpace* becomes *HisSpace,* how virtual community becomes true community, and how our lives point one another back to God.

So how do you do it? How can this become the way you live your life daily? The answer, once again, is with love.

CHAPTER SIX

On Earth as It Is in Heaven
The Christian Life from Here to Eternity

I love music of all kinds. Everything from baroque and classical to pop and classic rock has a place in my playlist. I think Mozart was a genius of the first order.

Music is a gift from God. It is one of the most precious blessings we have received from the Almighty.

I am always amazed by how beautifully diverse music can be. And although my musical tastes tend to be pretty broad, there is one particular song I'm not a big fan of. It's called "Big House," and I vividly remember the lyrics even though I haven't heard the song in over ten years. The music is fine. The tune is catchy. The beat is fun. There is nothing explicit or offensive in the song itself (in fact, the song is performed by a Christian band). No, my problem with the song stems from its description of eternity.

The song attempts to offer some thoughts and ideas about what things will be like after we die and go to heaven. It describes heaven as consisting of a big yard where the heavenly community can play football, a large table with an abundance of scrumptious food, and a big house with a surplus of nice, large rooms.

Now, I appreciate what the song is trying to do. It's attempting communicate the desirability of heaven and how wonderful the next life will be for all those who die in Christ. This is true and good. The next life will indeed be wonderful. Heaven will consist of delight beyond our wildest imagination. The song is right to a point: heaven will be great. However, this is also where the song falls short. It doesn't make heaven *great enough*.

We are programmed by God for something bigger than ourselves. We have been searching for happiness ever since we were little kids. Every decision we make, whether it's buying a toy, riding a bike, going to school, getting married, or starting a business is an attempt to find lasting happiness. Tragically, what so many people don't realize is that only in God will we ever find the lasting happiness we all crave.

If and when we make it to heaven, things like money, sex, football, and steak sandwiches (no matter how appealing now) will be the last things on our mind. Heaven is grounded in the life of God. God is the center of heaven. In him—and in him alone—will we find the happiness we spent our lives searching for. When we see and experience God as he is, money, sex, sports, and food won't be anything compared to the pleasure we will experience in God.

Our finite minds cannot even begin to imagine how wonderful heaven really is. St. Paul himself emphasizes this fact when he reminds us, "No eye has seen, nor ear heard, nor the heart of man conceived, what God has prepared for those who love him" (1 Corinthians 2:9; also see Isaiah 64:4).

THE NEXT LIFE

Several years ago I read a book by a famous author who was attempting to persuade his readers that this life is all there is—that there is no life after death. The only thing that mattered, he argued, was the here and now. Everyone is given a set number of years to live and after that, *nothing*. Game over. Thus, the author's point was simple: Live for today, because today may be all you get. Spend your every waking moment in search of the greatest thrills and earthly pleasures you can find, because this is all there is.

I remember being very depressed after reading that book. *Man, I thought to myself, if this is all that there is, then everything is meaningless.* The television, radio, and Internet are filled with accounts of evil and injustice and pain and suffering. If this life is all there is, then life is not a good thing—it's a curse.

Thanks be to God that this life isn't all that there is! There is life after death, and not just *any* life—the *greatest* life of all: the life of God himself. St. Paul was deeply committed to the reality of life after death. Everything he did—every breath, every step, every word—was motivated and inspired by his belief in the reality of heaven. He dreamt of heaven. He longed to be with his Savior, with the King himself, Jesus. The motto, the vision, and the inspiration of his life was the fact that, for him, "to live is Christ, and to die is gain" (Philippians 1:21).

St. Paul was torn between two worlds. He was torn between this world, this life, and the people who still hadn't met Jesus and the next world, where he could be with his Father and the glories of heaven. He spoke about this tension on several occasions. He shared how he was pulled in both directions. Paul shared that he desired to leave this world and be with Christ.

> For to me to live is Christ, and to die is gain. If it is to be life in the flesh, that means fruitful labor for me. Yet which I shall choose I cannot tell. I am hard pressed between the

two. My desire is to depart and be with Christ, for that is far better. But to remain in the flesh is more necessary on your account. Convinced of this, I know that I shall remain and continue with you all, for your progress and joy in the faith, so that in me you may have ample cause to glory in Christ Jesus. (Philippians 1:21–26)

This is one of the most moving passages we encounter in the writings of St. Paul. More than anything else, he desired final union with Jesus. He wanted to depart from this life so that he could pass into eternity and be with Christ, because "that is far better." I am almost moved to tears every time I read that verse.

First, what incredible love St. Paul must have had for his Savior! Everyone wants to be loved, and one of the most difficult things for those deeply in love is to be separated from each other. One of my friends—who is now happily married to the man of her dreams— recounts a time in their engagement when she and her fiancé had to live in different states for a few months. They did their best to keep in touch via telephone, letters, and occasional visits (this was back in the day before the Internet and email), but she shared how she was overcome with longing for her fiancé. This woman is not very dramatic—certainly not overly emotional—but she said that it was the first time in her life that she missed someone so much that it literally made her sick. The distance between them was so painful that she became physically ill.

This shouldn't surprise us. Love doesn't express itself in great distance and personal indifference. Quite the contrary: True love pulls at the deepest parts of our life and being and compels us to be united with the one we love. Love drives us to be with our beloved. Nothing is more difficult than separation from the person you love.

This is how St. Paul felt about his relationship with God. Now, obviously, he did not have any romantic feelings or sentiments for God in the same way that my friend had for her fiancé, but the apostle certainly felt a longing—an *aching*—for the one he loved more than life itself. Nothing was harder for St. Paul than being separated from his Lord. He endured many stonings, submitted to numerous whippings, and suffered from all forms of slander, starvation, and persecution for the sake of his beloved Jesus. And in the end, all he could think about was how much he yearned to be with Christ. The deepest longing of his heart was to be with Jesus. "My desire is to depart and be with Christ, for that is far better."

What amazing love! Although they churn out love story after love story, the greatest writers in Hollywood can't even begin to fathom a love like this!

This is the kind of love that "does not insist on its own way...is not irritable or resentful...[but rather] bears all things, believes all things, hopes all things, endures all things" (1 Corinthians 13:5–7). St. Paul's every action was done out of his profound love for Jesus. And he held on to the hope that even though he couldn't see God face-to-face here on earth—"for now we see in a mirror dimly"—he would, one day, be able to bask in the glory and presence of his Lord and Savior.

The second reason why I am almost brought to tears when I read this selection from Paul's writing is that *I often find my heart desiring something other than Christ.* I'm not like St. Paul on this point; sadly, there are a lot of other things that I often put ahead of Jesus and desire more than him.

How many of us would answer, "to be with Jesus in heaven," if we were randomly asked, "What do you want more than anything else?" Sadly, almost none of us. We are so caught up in the flashy lights and cool sounds of this fallen world that very few of us ever look up to heaven with wonder and longing. We all want things. We all have desires. That's part of what makes us human. The problem isn't that we have desires; the problem is that we desire all the wrong things.

WE SHOULD WANT MORE

A priest friend of mine was visiting a second-grade class at a Catholic elementary school. He decided to begin his visit by asking the children what they wanted to be when they grew up. "Does anyone want to be a priest or a nun?" he asked. The kids stared at him in silence. No answer was given. "Okay, does anyone want to be a nurse or a doctor?" Again, blank stares. The priest was thrown by their lack of response so he asked them "Well, then you tell me, what do you want to be when you grow up?" Without missing a beat, the entire class responded in unison: "I want to be rich!"

Sometimes it takes little children to speak the plain truth. We prefer the finite, small, temporal, passing, and (often) corrupt things of this world over the infinite splendor, joy, and eternal treasure available in heaven. How many of us go to bed at night dreaming and hoping for the joys of heaven? Rather, we go to bed hoping we will be able to enjoy ourselves next weekend or get invited to that party we heard our friends talking about or get the promotion we've been working for. These are the kinds of things that occupy our minds, take up our time, and rule our lives. This is so sad. Not because the things of this world are intrinsically evil; God made them, and they are good when used in their proper context. No, it is sad because we don't see how *infinitely more satisfying the presence of God is over the best parties and the most money this world has to offer.* That's what is tragic.

Our problem is not that we desire too much. Our problem is that we desire too *little.* Again, St. Paul reminds us: "No eye has seen, nor ear heard, nor the heart of man conceived, what God has prepared for those who love him" (1 Corinthians 2:9). We have no earthly idea just how unspeakably delightful heaven will be. God wishes to give us more than we could ever imagine. He wants to fill us with the greatest happiness, the fullest pleasure, and the most abundant joy. The Psalmist says that in God's "presence there is fullness of joy, and in his right hand are pleasures for evermore" (Psalms 16:11).

What an incredible statement! In God there is fullness of joy and pleasures for evermore. This is so counterintuitive. We tend to think of God and religion as impeding or preventing us from having joy and experiencing pleasure, but the Bible tells us that *the exact opposite is the case.* Only in God will our hearts find the joy and happiness they so desperately seek.

This is what St. Paul understood and what we habitually fail to recognize. We would much rather gorge ourselves with the rancid dumpster scraps the world throws at us than dine at the most elegant and satisfying feast Jesus has set before us. We are all looking for love, happiness, joy, pleasure—in all the wrong places.

Jesus is extending true love, true joy, and true pleasure to us. It's almost like he's saying, "Look, here you go! I have what you're looking for. I have what your soul is craving! Follow me, I will show you where you can find a joy, happiness, and pleasure that will last for all eternity!" And what do we do? We turn up our nose at his offer, shrug our shoulders in indifference, and walk away from what we need the most. What drives me to tears is that so many of us would rather have deformed, second-rate, fleeting pleasures than the infinite, the eternal, the everlasting and unchanging joy that God extends to us. How foolish can we be!

God wants us to be happy—he wants us to be happy more than *we* want to be happy. He knows what will truly satisfy us. He wants to lead us to the path of true happiness. But we turn him down; we walk away and prefer to feast on the scraps of this fallen world instead of from the immaculate table of our Father's heavenly banquet.

A Desperate Plea

I plead with you, if at this very moment you don't feel a deep longing to be with Christ, if the false and fleeting pleasures of this world are still more attractive to you than the infinite and lasting joys of heaven itself, put down this book, get on your knees, and ask God to help you see what is truly beautiful, what is truly desirable, what is truly satisfying. Pray, asking for eyes to see and a heart to love. And if you don't know what (or how) to pray, you can say something like this:

> Jesus, I know that only you are powerful enough to make me happy. I know that in you is found the fullness of joy and pleasures forevermore. But, sometimes, I don't desire you above all. Sometimes I get confused and buy into the lie that the fleeting pleasures of this world will give me more happiness than you.

Help me to see through this lie. Help me to remember that only in you will I find the happiness I seek. I'm not interested in a happiness that lasts a few seconds, a pleasure that lasts a few days, a joy that lasts a few years—or even a few hundred years!

No, Jesus, I want a joy and a happiness and a pleasure that will last ten billion years, and that will be only the very beginning. Jesus, I want you. Only you will give the happiness that never ends. Only you can satisfy the deepest longings of my heart. Only you can fill me with the joy that I so desperately seek. So here *I* am—poor and weak, broken and bruised—but desirous of the peace which never ends, the joy that is only found in and through you.

Fill me with your presence. Give me this happiness. I love you. Amen.

Nothing can compare with the joy of knowing and being united with Christ. Nothing else, no matter how great, lasting, significant, or powerful it may seem right now, can even begin to compare to the happiness that will come when we are united to Jesus in heaven. Everything else wanes in comparison to him.

This is why St. Paul could say, "My desire is to depart and be with Christ, for that is far better." Indeed, it is far better—union with Jesus is better than anything we could ever imagine.

OUR FINAL DESTINATION

The happiness and glory of heaven is the ultimate goal of all of reality. It is the treasure we are seeking. It is victory for which we are fighting. And, as St. Paul notes, it is the race we are running.

Do you not know that in a race all the runners compete, but only one receives the prize? So run that you may obtain it. Every athlete exercises self-control in all things. They do it to receive a perishable wreath, but we an imperishable. Well, I do not run aimlessly, I do not box as one beating the air; but I pommel my body and subdue it, lest after preaching to others I myself should be disqualified. (1 Corinthians 9:24–27)

It's amazing how hard people will work for something they consider valuable. Men and women devote their entire lives to accomplishing a handful of things. This is good. Things of great value are worth striving for. However, as great as earthly things may be, they will all pass away. No matter how sturdy your car, how up-to-date your computer, or how fit your body is right now, these will all eventually fail and be replaced by something else.

St. Paul eagerly desired that we not devote ourselves to the pursuit of temporal, passing goods. He wants us to commit our lives to pursuing the *eternal Good:* Jesus. We are in a race. We are running for the goal. We are fighting for the prize. However, unlike inanimate trophies which eventually lose value, our reward isn't an object or a possession—it's a person: Jesus. He is what we're fighting for; he is what we're pursuing. He is whom we're seeking.

The race can be challenging. As we've already noted in earlier chapters, this life is not easy. There are many times when we'd like to give up, throw in the towel, and call it quits. But St. Paul urges us to press on even through the most arduous trials. The reward is worth it. The difficulties are real, but the everlasting sweetness of victory will make all of the pains and struggles seem like nothing in comparison. The Christian life is hard—*really hard,* at times. But we press on "because of the hope laid up for [us] in heaven" (Colossians 1:5).

When our body begins to ache and our desires begin to wander away from heaven, we need to remain fixed on Jesus. St. Paul understood how challenging this can be. He reminded us that "while we are at home in the body we are away from the Lord, for we walk by faith, not by sight." And although "we would rather be away from the body and at home with the Lord" (2 Corinthians 5:6–8), we remain vigilant because "our common-wealth [citizenship] is in heaven," and we "await a Savior, the Lord Jesus Christ" (Philippians 3:20).

This world is not our home. We are mere sojourners here—we're just passing through. Our home is with Christ. We are citizens of heaven. Our unification in heaven was the plan from the very beginning. The apostle tells us that "[God] made known to us in all wisdom and insight the mystery of his will, according to his purpose which he set forth in Christ as a plan for the fullness of time, to unite all things in him, things in heaven and things on earth" (Ephesians 1:9–10). This was God's original plan. He didn't design the world to be a cosmic ant farm that he could watch and enjoy. He created us so that we could be united to him and experience his eternal happiness, joy, and pleasure. This is his desire. This is his plan.

The *Catechism of the Catholic Church* states that this unity with God is the very definition of heaven:

> This perfect life with the Most Holy Trinity—this communion of life and love with the Trinity, with the Virgin Mary, the angels and all the blessed—is called "heaven." Heaven is

the ultimate end and fulfillment of the deepest human longings, the state of supreme, definitive happiness. (CCC 1024)

Again, heaven does not consist of sports, large rooms, and tasty
food. Heaven consists of union with God. Heaven is being with
and in God for all eternity. Period. And while that might sound
boring to us here on earth, it's simply because we don't understand just who Jesus is. If we truly understood how wonderful
being with God in heaven really is, we would desire nothing
else—ever. Heaven is gazing upon the infinite splendor and glory
of God for all eternity.

Although it's impossible for us to imagine what that's like, one
day we will see God as he is. And we will be so enraptured by
his radiance that it will be the center of our attention. This vision
of God—seeing him face-to-face—that St. Paul alludes to in 1
Corinthians 13:12 is known as the *beatific vision*. It is the essence
of heaven. It is the source of our everlasting happiness.

A VOCATION OF LOVE

Each year, thousands of young people graduate from high school
and college. Finally, after hundreds of hours of study, research,
and classes, school is finally over. And while many of us experience great relief when we graduate, some of us are still haunted
by this terrifying question: "What am I going to do with my life?
I have a diploma. I've earned the degree. Now what?"

This is a very important question. It is a question of vocation.

Vocation isn't a common word in our modern time. It is rarely
used and often misunderstood. Usually, when we hear the word
vocation, we tend to think of people called to the priesthood
or religious life. While priests and religious certainly do have a

vocation, this is only part of the picture. What is often forgotten is this essential fact: *Everyone has a vocation.* No exceptions. While this may surprise you, it is absolutely true. Not everyone has a vocation to the priesthood or religious life, but everyone has a vocation to *love.*

The meaning of *vocation* is really simple: It is a divine calling. A vocation is what one is called by God to do with his or her life. It is where we find meaning and fulfillment. A vocation gives us purpose. The *Catechism of the Catholic Church* states that the fundamental "vocation of humanity is to show forth the image of God and to be transformed into the image of the Father's only Son" (CCC 1877).

Before anything else, we are called to be God's divinely adopted sons and daughters. God loves us so much that he not only forgives our sins but also incorporates us into his divine family. We are his children. This was his plan and desire from the very beginning. St. Paul states that "before the foundation of the world," God chose us and "destined us in love to be his sons" (Ephesians 1:4–5). God loved us so much that he called us to be his children. And it is only by fully embracing our heavenly Father's calling that we will find true, lasting happiness.

Sex won't give lasting happiness. Money can't purchase the joy we seek. Fame and power don't satisfy the deepest longings of our hearts. *These things—as good as they may be in their proper context—aren't powerful enough to give true happiness.* Only God is powerful enough make us eternally happy. Only he can satisfy our deepest longings.

Being a beloved child of God is the only thing that can give meaning to our lives. Life is difficult, and each individual vocation presents unique challenges and struggles. But we need not fear: We have a Father in heaven who has promised never to leave or forsake us in times of difficulty (see Hebrews 13:5). *Love is the key to sonship.* *God's love for us* is what makes us his divinely adopted children. *Our love for him is* what makes us willing to do whatever he asks.

Every vocation entails sacrifice. A husband has to sacrifice himself for his wife—he has to put his own individual interests and desires second to those of his spouse. A mother has to sacrifice herself for her children. She has to give up everything from her time and energy to her comfort and interests for the sake of her children. A priest sacrifices himself for the Church and his parish community. He gives up the great blessing of having a natural family in order to serve God's supernatural family.

Our heavenly Father has called us to love him and love those around us without holding anything back. We can't out-give God. The more we love—the more we *give*—the more we will receive. God is love (see 1 John 4:8). He is the source of all happiness. It is through loving others that we ourselves will be truly happy.

I meet a lot of young Catholics who think that the secret to happiness is meeting Mr. or Miss Right or becoming Father So-and-So. Vocations to marriage and the priesthood are indeed wonderful vocations with incalculable joys and blessings. However, vocations only work if we approach them by asking, "What can I give?" before we ask, "What can I get?" It is through giving that we receive. It is through dying to self that we truly find life. It is through serving others that we are strengthened. And it is only through this kind of love—lived here on earth and perfected in heaven—that we will find the happiness which never ends.

We need to follow St. Paul in making love our "aim" (1 Corinthians 14:1). Everything we do needs to be firmly "rooted and grounded in love" (Ephesians 3:17) so that we might be fully united to Jesus in heaven. God is love—it is who he is; it is what he does. May we all be imitators of him! May we love here on earth as our heavenly Father loves eternally in heaven.

It is important to remember that love doesn't begin in heaven; it has to start in our hearts here on earth. But we can also take great comfort in the fact that love doesn't end after our time in this world is over; it is only just beginning.

Enduring Love

Things will be different in heaven. You won't get tired. Sleep will no longer be needed. Fun and games won't be as important to you. There will be no sadness. No crying. No weeping or mourning. Heaven is full of infinite joy and happiness. All the things that concerned and worried you here on earth will no longer be a source of anxiety. The only thing that will be at the center of your heavenly life is love.

In one of his most famous chapters, St. Paul describes the nature of love and speaks of it like this:

> Love never ends; as for prophecies, they will pass away; as for tongues, they will cease; as for knowledge, it will pass away. For our knowledge is imperfect and our prophecy is imperfect; but when the perfect comes, the imperfect will pass away.... For now we see in a mirror dimly, but then face to face. Now I know in part; then I shall understand fully, even as I have been fully understood. So faith, hope, love abide, these three; but the greatest of these is love. (1 Corinthians 13:8–13)

Let's look at this significant passage very carefully. The apostle begins by noting that "love never ends." This is striking, because there are a lot of things that will end when we get to heaven. Sin does not exist in heaven. When you're in the presence of God—enveloped in his glory and love—sinful thoughts and actions will be impossible. You will be so caught up in his beauty and splendor, no evil thought will enter your mind, even for a split second. Your earthly concerns and fears will vanish. Your difficulties and confusion will be resolved. When you see your heavenly Father as he is in all his glory, love is the only thing that will remain. Nothing else will matter. Nothing else will occupy your mind or grab your attention. God—and God alone—will be your joy and your delight.

"Love never ends." It is amazing that, of all the things here on earth, love is the only thing that will remain constant from this life into the next life. St. Paul notes that right now "our knowledge is imperfect…. We see in a mirror dimly." God is so much greater than we are that our frail human minds can't perceive and understand his splendor. That's why we need faith. Faith is a gift from God that enables us to know things which surpass our natural abilities.

For example, I don't need faith to believe that two plus two equals four. Why? Because my mind can understand this simple equation. Simple arithmetic is not above my mind's capability. I can understand that two plus two equals four without supernatural assistance. However, the doctrine of the Trinity does require faith. Why? Because this is something that a human mind would never be able to figure out on its own. A human mind can solve a simple math problem, but a human mind cannot solve the mystery of God being Father, Son, and Holy Spirit—three in one.

God had to reveal this truth to us. He knew that we would never figure it out on our own, so he revealed it through the Bible and the teachings of the Church. We believe that the Trinity is true not because we fully understand it, but because God told us it is true. This is the definition of supernatural faith—believing something we can't figure out on our own because God reveals it to us.

Faith exists here on the earth. I don't see God face-to-face here and now. I don't see Jesus in the Eucharist. My human eyes aren't powerful enough to discern his divine presence. Is he really there? Yes! Do I believe it? Absolutely! However, faith will not exist in heaven. Belief will no longer be necessary when we're united with God in his heavenly kingdom.

Why is this? Why does faith exist on earth and not in heaven? The answer is simple: When we're in heaven, we will be able to *see* God as he is. Right now, I can't see God directly. Therefore I have faith—I believe what God has said but I cannot see. When I'm in heaven, however, I won't have to believe it.

I'll know it. When I'm in heaven, I will be able to see God for myself; faith will no longer be necessary. As St. Paul says, "Now I know in part; then I shall understand fully" (1 Corinthians 13:12).

Hope is another thing that exists on earth but does not exist in heaven. When I hope for something, I desire something that I do not yet possess. When I say, "I hope I get an A on my math test," I mean that I have not yet received an A on my test. We hope for things that we do not have. We hope for things that we wish to obtain.

However, when we're in heaven, we will no longer have to hope for the glory of Christ because we will be in Christ's glorious presence. It will no longer be far off, in the future. When we're in heaven, we will possess the infinite joy and happiness we spend our whole lives hoping to attain—we will finally have it. Like faith, hope only exists on earth. When we get to heaven faith and hope will disappear because we will see God as he is and have the joy that is only found in him.

Faith ends. Hope ends. But "love never ends." In fact, rather than disappearing, once we enter into the glories of heaven, love finds its ultimate perfection. It doesn't stop once we get to heaven; it gets even better! Love is supreme because it is *permanent*. We won't be the least bit disappointed that heaven is not a big house full of rooms, food, and football games. We will be overcome with the everlasting pleasure and delight of being enveloped in God's love. It's just like St. Paul so beautifully states: "Faith, hope, love abide, these three; but the greatest of these is love."

CHAPTER SEVEN

Choose Your Own Adventure
The Practicality of St. Paul

I mentioned in the introduction that my favorite book to look at was my family's Catholic picture Bible. My favorite books to *actually read* were from a series called *Choose Your Own Adventure.* Some of you might remember them. Every page offered you a particular situation and two choices. One choice led you to one page, the other choice led you to a different page, and each page contained more choices and so on. Your story (adventure) ended differently and at different times, depending upon what you chose on the previous page. It was a nice metaphor for life, even if I didn't know at the time what a metaphor was. I just liked the empowerment of making choices at such a young age. I liked the notion of controlling my destiny.

God gives you free will. Your life is in your hands. Additionally, allowing his life to work through you (or not) is your decision. Saul had an encounter with Christ, and then he had a choice to make. He chose to serve God. Next came the choice of whether or not to change his approach to faith, and he said yes. Next came the calling to preach in Christ's name. Again, he said yes.

Paul's life story was really a choose your own adventure of sorts. He was faced with decision after decision to choose himself or choose Christ. Your life is no different. Today you will be given the choice of whether to live for God or for yourself (see Deuteronomy 30:15–20). You'll probably be given several opportunities to choose between God and self during the course of your day. Let's say that the new adventure of your life starts right now.

So the question is this: how far are you willing to go for God?

How Far Are You Willing to Go?

Following this paragraph are ten questions. The questions are straightforward and seem simple enough. Saying yes to each is easy, but living yes on a daily basis is quite difficult. St. Paul had to answer each of these questions, internally first before living them externally. His life became a living proclamation of his yes to each. If your response to each one is also yes, continue reading. If your response to one (or several) of the questions is no, we encourage you to stop reading and spend some time in prayer, asking the Holy Spirit to open your mind and heart to the areas that need to change in your life right now.

Are you willing to be uncomfortable for God?

Are you willing to trust God completely?

Are you willing to surrender your plans and your life to God?

Are you willing to be honest with God about your sin?

Are you willing to change sinful environments and relationships in order to live a more holy life?

Are you willing to personally sacrifice so that others might know Christ?

Are you willing to try new things in your prayer life, home life, parish life, school life and/or work life?

Are you willing to seek God proactively and urgently?

Are you willing to protect your state of grace more vigilantly?

Are you willing to share God's grace with *everyone*?

Notice that these questions all say "willing," not "able." The apostles and saints weren't able to do anything heroic or miraculous by themselves without the power of Christ and the Holy Spirit. By ourselves we are nothing, but with the Holy Spirit, St. Paul reminds us that we "can do all things" (Philippians 4:13).

St. Paul understood that he was nothing without God, but that with God he was powerful beyond measure. His whole life became an attempt to allow God's life to overtake and consume his life. As we stated in the introduction, St. Paul wasn't writing or preaching another Gospel. For Paul, it wasn't about recording or retelling what Jesus said or did; it was about *living and becoming what Christ said to do,* daily and in practical ways.

In this final chapter, we're going to take a *very brief* look at each of these ten questions and discuss in *practical terms* what each ones means to you and to your daily faith walk.

Remember, this is your adventure. You get to choose if you move on to the next question or not. Your honest response should dictate if you continue reading or pause to pray. To quote *Indiana Jones and the Last Crusade,* "Choose wisely."

1. ARE YOU WILLING TO BE UNCOMFORTABLE FOR GOD?

Remember Saul's conversion? Remember what all he went through? Ever wonder what kept Paul going for so many miles and for so many years?

Five times I have received at the hands of the Jews the forty lashes less one. Three times I have been beaten with rods; once I was stoned. Three times I have been shipwrecked; a night and a day I have been adrift at sea; on frequent journeys in danger from rivers, danger from robbers, danger from my own people, danger from Gentiles, danger in the city, danger in the wilderness, danger at sea, danger from false brethren; in toil and hardship, through many a sleepless night, in hunger and thirst, often without food, in cold and exposure. And, apart from other things, there is the daily pressure upon me of my anxiety for all the churches. (2 Corinthians 11:24–28)

So why did he keep at it? Why didn't he just set up shop in Damascus, writing letters and waiting for people to come to him to hear him preach? The simple answer would be that Jesus himself went out to the sinners and outcasts. That, in turn, is what an apostle is: one who is sent forth. That answer is correct, but to say it is the only reason would be selling Paul short. No, for Paul it wasn't just occupational, it was personal.

Paul was used to living out his religious beliefs; he was a Pharisee. After experiencing the mercy of Christ firsthand, however, Paul's attitude *changed*. *Now it* wasn't just about the *what* of his religion—it was about the *who*.

You should have the same goal. Your Catholic faith ought to be about a relationship with God, not just *participation* in the Church.

When your faith is centered around God, everything changes. You'll go to Mass out of love, not obligation. You'll serve with joy, not out of guilt. You'll confess your sins because of your desire to grow in holiness, not just to avoid hell.

When your faith is personal, you're willing to be uncomfortable because you're in relationship with God. When it's cold and impersonal, every sacrifice has the potential of creating bitterness or resentment within your soul. Base your faith on a personal, intimate relationship with Jesus Christ, and watch how comfortable you'll get being uncomfortable.

If you can say yes to being uncomfortable for God, move on to the next question. If you are unwilling to be uncomfortable *for* God, spend some time in prayer before moving on.

2. ARE YOU WILLING TO TRUST GOD COMPLETELY?

Trust might be the one area that every Christian struggles with the most. We have an easy time telling others to trust God, but when it comes to trusting him ourselves, we are reluctant to let go of control and let God be God. Trusting in God requires (and challenges) the theological virtues of faith, hope, and love. These are not merely intellectual; each virtue properly lived out necessitates action on our part. We demonstrate what we believe by our actions. Actions follow beliefs.

Consider this famous story:

> A huge crowd was watching the famous tightrope walker, Blondin, cross Niagara Falls one day in 1860. He crossed it numerous times—a 1,000 foot trip, 160 feet above the raging waters. He not only walked across it; he also pushed a wheelbarrow across it.
>
> One little boy just stared in amazement. So after completing a crossing, [Blondin] looked at that little boy and said, "Do you believe I could take a person across in the wheelbarrow without falling?"

"Yes, sir. I really do."

The fellow says, "Well then, get in, son."[17]

It's not enough to say you trust God or to tell others to trust him. Are you willing to put your money where your mouth is and get into his wheelbarrow?

In order to grow in your faith, you must trust God, for he is the means and the end of your pursuit. If this is a struggle for you, you must at least be willing to admit to him that you struggle in this area; even admitting it is, in essence, a sign of your trust in his mercy.

Tell God that you don't understand everything he has planned for you, but that you trust him. Tell Jesus you are scared but that you want to trust him more completely. Invite Christ into your life, job, future, relationship, marriage, friendships—and then surrender control. He didn't promise us it would be easy, but he did promise us that he is closer than we might think, more aware than we might give him credit for, and more loving than we can possibly comprehend.

If you trust God, move on to the next question. If you struggle with trust, pray honestly about this before moving on.

3. ARE YOU WILLING TO SURRENDER YOUR PLANS AND YOUR LIFE TO GOD?

What does a trusting relationship look like? Saying "I trust you" is easy (or maybe not, depending how you responded to the previous question), but moving beyond the words and living out "I trust you, God" in action is challenging. How do you get to a point where God is in control of your life instead of you controlling your life and simply asking God to agree with your plans?

That's where we go wrong much of the time: We look at our lives as our own. We forget to factor our creator into the equation. We ignore the author of our stories. The divine author has a story written for you, however—and it's time you prayerfully opened up to it.

God is pro-life in the obvious sense (anti-murder and abortion), and also in the less obvious sense: He has an expectation that we will bear fruit (see Genesis 1:28; John 15:16). God created you for good works (Ephesians 2:10). Likewise, God created you with a purpose that only *you* can fulfill (see Jeremiah 1:4–8). You have a mission designed specifically for you, as we talked about in the last chapter.

Often we fear saying yes to God because we don't trust where he is going to take us. We're afraid that his plan is going to be boring, too hard, or the opposite of what we want. St. Paul reminds us that with God we have nothing to fear (see 2 Timothy 1:7). His plan is better than ours (see Jeremiah 29:11–12). God will take care of you, so put your trust in him. In the end, you'll not only be faithful, you'll be more joyful, too. He won't steer you wrong, ever.[18]

If you will surrender your plans in favor of God's plans, move on to the next question. If there are plans you're not ready to let go of, pray about this before moving on.

4. ARE YOU WILLING TO BE HONEST WITH GOD ABOUT YOUR SIN? Do you play hide and seek with God? Adam did, and look where it got him. Do you think you can hide your sins from God? Even if you have successfully hidden sins from everyone else in your life until now, God knows. He knows the worst thing you've ever done (the thing that maybe your friends and family don't even

know about), and he sees the best you can be through him (something that you might not even realize yourself).

Christ is waiting to forgive and heal you, not waiting to condemn you. Don't pretend the sin isn't there. Don't fool yourself into thinking that just because the rest of your life might appear perfect to the world God sees it the same way.

Are you *real* with Jesus? Do you invite Jesus into every corner of your life? Not just the polished rooms that you are proud to display, but the darkest recesses of your soul? Do you let Jesus roll up his sleeves and get to work on those corners of your spiritual house that remain cluttered, dirty, or just plain untouchable? Do you invite him into your soul's garage, let him see the attic, or invite him to root around in the closets of your soul, cluttered with sin, failure, and shame?19

Jesus was born into a messy manger. Jesus died on a messy cross. He rose again to conquer your mess. Jesus isn't afraid of your mess. Don't be afraid of his grace, healing, and forgiveness. If you are authentic and transparent with God, move on to the next question. If you feel ashamed and feel resistance to letting him into your whole heart, spend some time in prayer asking him to help you.

5. ARE YOU WILLING TO CHANGE SINFUL ENVIRONMENTS AND RELATIONSHIPS IN ORDER TO LIVE A MORE HOLY LIFE?

Have you ever thought to yourself, I feel like such a failure.... I just keep confessing the same sins?

If so, you're not alone; the greatest saints had the same struggle. Eventually, though, virtue won out for them, and it can for you, too.

Too often we deal with the effects of sin, but not its roots. It's like we are drowning in a river and the priest (Christ) keeps pulling us out (confession). It's not until we are on dry ground and proactively walk upstream to find the source of the water (sin) that we can really do anything about it. As an example, for some people the river is drunkenness, but the source is an addiction to alcohol. For others the sin is masturbation, but the source is an addiction to pornography. The further upstream we walk, the deeper we find the root causes of those addictions—fear, loneliness, depression, anger, abandonment, low self-esteem, and so on. At times your body and soul are immersed in a deadly and painful tug-of-war, and you feel helpless in the battle. St. Paul knew the conflict all too well:

> I do not understand my own actions. For I do not do the thing that I want, but I do the very thing that I hate.... So then it is no longer I that do it, but sin which dwells in me. (Romans 7:15–17)

It's not enough to recognize the sins we commit, we must prayerfully seek out the source. If we don't get to the root of our sin, our flesh and spirit will be in constant battle. True freedom means first locating the sources of our sin and then surrendering them to Christ. It is in that surrender that you will finally taste true freedom.

> For those who live according to the flesh set their minds on the things of the flesh, but those who live according to the Spirit set their minds on the things of the Spirit. To set the mind on the flesh is death, but to set the mind on the Spirit is life and peace. (Romans 8:5–6)

Be aware: The minute you start asking questions—such as, "Where does my sin come from?" or, "How can I eliminate these sins, Lord?"—you will be attacked. Paul reminds us of this later in Romans: "When I want to do right, evil is at hand (Romans 7:21)." The devil doesn't want you to realize these sources of sin, as they are his greatest weapon against you and the means by which he keeps us enslaved to sin and suffocated in his grip.

If you are willing to let God remove and destroy sinful relationships and environments in your life, move on to the next question. If there are areas of sin you're not ready to give up, ask God to change your heart before moving on.

6. ARE YOU WILLING TO PERSONALLY SACRIFICE SO THAT OTHERS MIGHT KNOW CHRIST?

What are you willing to do for God in order to better live out your faith? How far are you willing to go?

Let's find out.

Would you get rid of your Internet? Television? iPod?

Would you stop listening to any CDs that don't lead you closer to God?

Would you get rid of your video games?

Would you break up with your boyfriend/girlfriend?

Would you stop abusing your sexuality?

Would you never look at pornography again?

Would you go to counseling with your husband/wife?

Would you forgive *all those* who have hurt you?

Would you seek forgiveness from all those you have hurt?

Would you stop drinking alcohol?

Would you never touch drugs again?

Would you invite your neighbors, classmates, or coworkers to Church?

Would you reach out to the least popular people around you? Would you offer friendship to those who most irritate or annoy you?

Would you change your college major?

Would you change or quit your job?

Would you check out a seminary or convent?

Would you give away most of your clothes?

Would you arrange your schedule to get to Adoration every day?

Would you move to another country to tell people about Jesus?

Would you donate your time to do service once a week?

Of course, there are certain things on this list you shouldn't be doing anyway (like using drugs or looking at pornography). The bigger question is whether anything on this list is difficult for you to say no to doing. Is there anything here that you just can't do or (more to the point) won't do for God? Are you willing to sacrifice, personally, until it hurts?

Commit the following two verses to memory. Pray them every time you pass a crucifix. Pray them every time you see the body of Christ elevated at Mass. Pray them every time you feel tempted to be selfish. Pray them every time you are tempted sexually. Pray them every time someone makes you feel foolish for believing this fairy tale message of Christ in the twenty-first century.

> I appeal to you therefore, brethren, by the mercies of God, to present your bodies as a living sacrifice, holy and acceptable to God, which is your spiritual worship. Do not be conformed to this world but be transformed by the renewal

of your mind, that you may prove what is the will of God, what is good and acceptable and perfect." (Romans 12:1–2)

If you are willing to sacrifice (even if it hurts), move on to the next question. If you are resistant to this idea, pray about it more before moving on.

7. ARE YOU WILLING TO TRY NEW THINGS IN YOUR PRAYER LIFE, HOME LIFE, PARISH LIFE, SCHOOL LIFE AND/OR WORK LIFE?

Rethinking Your Prayer Life

Why pray? Seriously, why do you pray? Is it to get things from God? Is it to change the way things are going in your life? Is it to thank God and worship him? Is it to become more like Christ? Is it to understand God better, or is it to get him to understand you better? Be honest.

Practically speaking, prayer becomes more challenging the less you do it. The more you try, the more you practice, the more time you actually set aside to do it, the more comfortable you'll become with it.

Prayer is the great gift of our existence. Prayer is the ability to step out of yourself and your circumstances; it's the ability to leave behind the frustrations and anxieties of the day and just throw yourself into the arms of God. Consider what these saintly souls had to say about prayer:[20]

> Prayer is the best weapon we possess, the key that opens the heart of God.
>
> —St. Padre Pio

> Change your hearts.... Unless we change our hearts we are not converted. Changing places is not the answer. The

answer is to change our hearts. And how do we change? By praying.

—Mother Teresa

How to pray? This is a simple matter. I would say: Pray any way you like, so long as you do pray.

—Pope John Paul II

Often the mere babblings of a child will touch his father in heaven.

—St. John of the Ladder

Lord, teach me to seek you, and reveal yourself to me as I look for you. For I cannot seek you unless you first teach me.

—St. Ambrose

Prayer is the place of refuge for every worry, a foundation for cheerfulness, a source of constant happiness, a protection against sadness.

—St. John Chrysostom

Souls without prayer are like bodies, palsied and lame, having hands and feet they cannot use.

—St. Teresa of Avila

However softly we speak, he is near enough to hear us.

—St. Teresa of Avila

Do not distress yourself about your prayers. It is not always necessary to employ words, even inwardly, it is enough to raise your heart and let it rest in our Lord.

—St. Francis de Sales

We must pray literally without ceasing—without ceasing; in every occurrence…a habit of lifting up the heart to God, as in a constant communication with Him.

—St. Elizabeth Seton

You don't know how to pray? Put yourself in the presence of God, and as soon as you have said, 'Lord, I don't know how to pray!' you can be sure you have already begun.

—St. Josemaría Escrivá

The Church offers us so many different forms of prayer—some free-form, some more focused. No matter how awake or tired your mind, no matter how alert or fatigued your heart, there is always a form of prayer available to lead you deeper into the tireless heart of God.

Adoration of the Blessed Sacrament, the rosary, the Liturgy of the Hours, journaling, praise and worship, sacred silence, *lectio divina*, the Stations of the Cross, and fasting are all forms of prayer that can transform the mundane life into encounters with God's grace. When all else fails, never doubt the power of simply praying and calling upon the name of Jesus; that alone, praying the name above all names (see Philippians 2:10–14), is one of the greatest prayers we can ever pray.

Discover different forms of prayer, and break out of any spiritual ruts that may creep into your prayer life. Most importantly, commit yourself to daily prayer, praying the Scriptures, and frequenting the sacraments.

Rethinking Your Home Life

It is usually a lot harder to be a good Christian in our own homes or around our own friends than it is around strangers. Those closest to see us at our worst...all those times that we don't act very Christian, those times that we are selfish, rude, or impatient. Some people feel it is okay to scream at their spouses or children because families have to love you anyway. Others feel it is okay to scream at the world because who cares if they love you back?

In either case, we would be shortsighted to think that such conduct is admissible or encouraged by Christ. If you can't envision Joseph screaming at Mary or Mary yelling at Jesus, it's a good rule of thumb that it's not what Jesus would want you to do, either. Think about it.

You have been purchased at a great price, as St. Paul reminds us in 1 Corinthians 6:20. You have been called to live the Gospel, beginning in your own home. Try to do this nonverbally more often than verbally. Come up with a list of little ways you can show love in your home. Especially think of things that stretch you, things that might hurt a little at first...things that will take a shot at your pride. Then do them!

Your example of Christ (at home and abroad) should be like St. Paul's. Your faith needs to be:

Practical, so people can relate
Relevant, to affect peoples' lives daily
Simple, so people will remember
Personal, to show that you know Christ
Joyful, to be attractive
Real, to speak the truth with authenticity

Yes, some people will think you're nuts, but then again, some won't. Don't worry about what people think. God's thoughts (see Isaiah 55:8–9) are the only thoughts that are truly important.

Rethinking Your Parish Life

One of the places we most clearly see our Christian solidarity is the Holy Mass, the Liturgy. If someone says, "I'm a Christian, but I just don't believe in organized religion. Why can't I just pray alone?", St. Paul's response would be, "You *can and should* pray alone—never cease praying," but true Christians understand that they are "members one of another" (Romans 12:5) and that "none of us lives to himself" (Romans 14:7). We should never neglect or reject the gathering together of God's people in worship (see Hebrews 12:25). Everything I do affects the rest of the living body of Christ. Everything that you do affects the body, too, for better or for worse.

Since we are so intimately connected and our souls and lives are so intertwined in this mystical body of Christ, it is only natural that we would (and should) worship *together* (see Matthew 18:20). Worship is the most intimate expression of our love for God, a humble and passionate response to his sovereignty. Read the Acts of the Apostles; the early Christians worshiped together. Their example is meaningful, essential, and timeless.

How connected would we *truly* be to the body of Christ if we desired to be separate and alone when we worship? The same perspective applies to other elements of living as one body. Do you tithe to your parish? Do you participate in Church functions? Do you engage in the community, or do you run for the parking lot following Mass? Are you serving within the parish community? Are you involved in a ministry?

If we are *truly one body* as St. Paul challenges us to be, these questions need to be asked, and if necessary, perspectives and practices need to change. Take a hard look at how you approach your time at your local parish, and ask yourself if there is something more you could be doing for the kingdom.

Rethinking Your School Life or Work Life

Whether you are still in school or are part of the full-time working world, rethinking this aspect of your life is often like rethinking your diet—you know you need to make some changes, but you really don't want to make them. Let's focus on what God might desire from you in these places. There are souls he wants to touch through your example.

To be honest, God has probably already revealed to you the people in these settings who most need Christ. Here are some to consider:

At School

That girl in class who is the most quiet usually has some of the most meaningful things to say, but she is probably fearful to say them for a variety of reasons. Reach out to her.

That guy in class who is always sarcastic or cutting is usually the one who is most insecure, and he tries to hide that fact in the process. Reach out to him.

At Work

That man in the office who is the most outspoken and opinionated professionally is usually the least confident personally. Model humility.

That woman in the office who is the most forward or immodest on the exterior is usually the most wounded on the interior. Affirm her interior.

These examples are not meant to dismiss the hurtful actions of others, but merely offer a different perspective on people whose lives and decisions might make your faith walk a little more challenging. We're called to be Christ even when the people we're trying to help ignore, reject, and ridicule us. Be prepared: this lifestyle of radical love is not easy, but it's infinitely worth it.

If you truly commit yourself to being Christ to all people, you will face many struggles and great opposition. But don't be afraid. Both Jesus and St. Paul knew what it was like to be rejected by those you love, and this is why the apostle tells us to stand firm in our commitment to the high road of love, "living a life worthy of the call you have received" (Ephesians 4:1).

Are you willing to do things differently? Are you willing to approach God differently? Are you willing to approach your family members with more love and understanding? Are you willing to lead more by your example of holiness?

If you are willing to radically change your prayer life, home life, parish life, and school/work life, move on to the next question. If you are struggling in these areas, spend some time in reflection and prayer before moving on.

8. ARE YOU WILLING TO SEEK GOD MORE PROACTIVELY AND MORE URGENTLY?

As we mentioned earlier, the sacraments are the most perfect encounter of Christ's grace that the Church has to offer. The sacraments were instituted by Christ himself, and two of them specifically are especially important for us to be able to live out this Christian life that St. Paul points us toward: the Eucharist and reconciliation.

Think about rearranging your schedule so you encounter Christ's grace in the sacraments more regularly and more intentionally. Doing so would include:

Going to daily Mass

Spending at least an hour a week in Adoration of the Blessed Sacrament

Frequenting the sacrament of reconciliation at least once a month

Praying the Sunday readings in the days prior to Mass, in order to be prepared

Remember, it wasn't until St. Paul encountered Christ personally (as we now do in the sacraments) that he could fulfill his vocation. St. Paul didn't just encounter Christ once, but constantly, in the Eucharist.

St. Paul *vehemently defended* the Real Presence of Jesus in the Eucharist (see 1 Corinthians 11:23–29). And even though St. Paul wasn't present at the Last Supper, he fully received (and, in turn, handed on) the *living tradition* of the Eucharistic sacrifice, safeguarded by the apostolic tradition (see 2 Thessalonians 2:15). The bread is not mere bread. The wine is not mere wine. It is nothing less that Jesus himself—full and complete: *body and blood, soul and divinity.*

The Catholic Church has always taught that Christ died once and for all as "a single sacrifice for sins" (Hebrews 10:12). Thus the Church *does not teach that we are re-sacrificing Jesus Christ during Mass.* Christ's loving sacrifice on the Cross over two thousand years ago can never be repeated—it's impossible to repeat something that never ended. In addition, the effects of that loving sacrifice will never be exhausted. Thus, the Mass does not re-sacrifice Jesus, but it does *represent* (re-present) his one sacrifice, enabling us to receive the fullness of his loving presence.

St. Paul felt so strongly about the fact that the bread and wine were *truly* transubstantiated into Christ's flesh and blood, that he strictly warned followers who were in a state of serious (mortal) sin, not to partake, lest they eat and drink judgment unto themselves (see 1 Corinthians 11:27–29). We dare not receive Jesus's holy presence in the Eucharist unless his divine life (his grace) is present in our souls.

Jesus commanded us to celebrate the Mass in "remembrance" of him (see Luke 22:19–20). He commanded us to become one *with* him through the Eucharist. We intimately become one with Christ, again and again, through the sacraments; this is what it truly means to be re-membered by God—to be filled with the fullness of his divine life and presence.

To state things clearly, it's not so much a matter of us consuming *Christ* as it is of Christ consuming *us* in the Eucharist. He is received into us, and *we* are received *into* him. What a glorious mystery this is! How incredible it is that we, mere humans, are blessed enough to partake of God's own divine nature (see 2 Peter 1:4). How loved we are to become one with God and have our lives joined to his!

St. Paul did not believe that the Eucharist is merely a *symbol.* He believed that it was really *Jesus.* This is why he took the Eucharist so seriously in his writings, and this is why *we* need to take his writings about the Eucharist very seriously in our lives. Paul wasn't the only saint who proclaimed Christ's true presence in the Eucharistic sacrifice, either. St. Cyril of Jerusalem, St. Irenaeus, St. Justin Martyr, St. Augustine—all four of these famous early Church fathers (and countless more) have attested to the real presence of Christ in the Eucharist.

It may look like typical bread, it may taste like simple wine, but it is nothing less than the body and blood of our sovereign Lord, Jesus Christ. St. Paul reminded us that "as often as you eat this bread and drink the cup, you proclaim the Lord's death until he comes" (1 Corinthians 11:26).

If you desire to become more sacramental, move on to the next question. If the sacraments don't seem all that important to you, spend some time in prayer before moving on.

9. ARE YOU WILLING TO PROTECT YOUR STATE OF GRACE MORE VIGILANTLY?

The Catholic Church teaches that we need to be in a state of grace prior to receiving the Eucharist. In other words, if we have committed a mortal sin, we should not receive Communion without first going to confession. This is because sin threatens and destroys our state of grace.

Now, how do you change your approach in such a way that you are not only trying to avoid sin but *preserving your state of grace*? How do you stay rooted in Christ and protect your state of grace in the face of temptation? St. Paul told the Colossian believers:

> As therefore you received Christ Jesus the Lord, so live in him, rooted and built up in him.... See to it that no one makes a prey of you by philosophy and empty deceit, according to human tradition, according to the elemental spirits of the universe, and not according to Christ. (Colossians 2:6–8)

We must go to Christ if we want to be built up in him. Through our justification in Christ and our ongoing sanctification through the Holy Spirit, we can boldly and confidently approach the throne of God's grace and receive grace and mercy (see Hebrews

4:16). God's mercy is limitless and his love is unconditional. He desires for us to know, have, and seek his grace, so that we might live more in his image, the image of the Incarnation.

It's by God's grace that we go from being slaves to being free (see Romans 6:17–23). It's by God's grace that we move from death to life (Romans 6:13). It's by God's grace that you can make it through your day, each day. It's by God's grace that you go from living an ordinary life to living an extraordinary life.

It's by God's grace that prayer becomes passionate, the sacraments become intimate, and Mary's heart was made immaculate. It's by God's grace that you can become a saint.

If you are committed to protecting your state of grace, move on to the next question. If you don't see the point, pray about it more before moving on.

10. Are you willing to share God's grace with everyone?
God thinks more highly of you than you do of yourself. He believes in you. He believes in your potential. God doesn't just love you, he likes you! He doesn't always like everything you do, but he never stops liking you. How do I know? Because he created you, uniquely, and he redeemed you, personally.

God liked Saul, too, and that's why God didn't give up on him, even when he was killing Christians. God remembers something that our fickle human brains always seem to forget…that he (God) can do more with a penitent sinner than he can with a "saintly" person who doesn't feel they have any need of his mercy.

I am a sinner. So are you. I'm called to be a saint. So are you.

So, how do we do it? We don't…God's grace does. All you have to do is let God be God…in you.

Sinners focus on self, saints on others.

Sinners focus on their wants, saints on what God wants.

Sinners, though, can and do become saints.

With the exception of the Blessed Virgin Mary, every saint began as a sinner. Saints call out to sinners.

Saints are more aware of their sin than their saintliness.

Saints focus more on God's grace than their own sin.

Focus more on your output than your input. Focus more on serving others than on how others can serve you. Remember how Jesus washed the disciples' feet before the Last Supper? The more you seek Jesus in the Word, the sacraments, and prayer, the more you avail yourself of that divine "input," the more power and grace you'll have to offer the world via your output. See how it works? St. Paul did. He served the body with every breath until his dying breath. That's how the sinner became the saint—he let God's life overtake his own life, and it overflowed to everyone God put in his path.

If you are willing to share God's grace with *everyone*, finish reading. If you are scared to share your faith with others, ask God to give you a holy boldness before moving on.

St. Paul Believes in Christ's Presence in You

Even if you don't see Christ in yourself, you can bet that St. Paul would have seen and affirmed Christ in you! That's what the eyes of faith do, they see as God sees, not as man sees (1 Samuel 16:7). St. Paul would not only affirm your goodness but also remind you of how good you are designed to be. He would remind you that God sees you as beautiful and glorious and good.

Paul would never give up on you as others might do. He would never give up on you as you might give up on yourself. Ask St. Paul to pray for you now.

St. Paul's intercessory prayer on your behalf is powerful. Ask him to join his prayers to your prayers as you lay them at the feet of Jesus Christ.

Believe in your goodness and in your holiness in Christ. Share that holiness with others, and their hearts will, over time, be convicted to change as well. Your example will call them to holiness in their own lives. If you don't know how to seek holiness, it's simple: "Seek first his kingdom and his righteousness" (Matthew 6:33) in every decision, big and small. That is the challenge that makes life such an adventure. Make no mistake, you're not choosing God—he has already chosen you (see John 15:16)! God is calling you to respond.

St. Paul didn't just see Christ on the road one day. St. Paul, like countless saintly souls who came after him, saw Christ every day. He knew something that too many modern Christians (yes, even Catholics) proclaim but seem to forget, namely: Christ is living and active.

Christ's Word is living and active. His sacraments and Church are living and active. And *you* are designed to be living *and* active, too. He created you to *live*, not just breathe—living in right relationship with God in the life of his Son (justification) and actively loving in power of his Spirit (sanctification).

So, as you reach the end of this book, consider how you, like St. Paul, might turn a new page in your walk with Christ, and to quote our older brother in the faith one last time:

Put on then, as God's chosen ones, holy and beloved, compassion, kindness, lowliness, meekness, and patience, forbearing one another and, if one has a complaint against another, forgiving each other; as the Lord has forgiven you, so you also must forgive. And above all these put on love, which binds everything together in perfect harmony. And let the peace of Christ rule in your hearts, to which indeed you were called in the one body. And be thankful. Let the word of Christ dwell in you richly, teach and admonish one another in all wisdom, and sing psalms and hymns and spiritual songs with thankfulness in your hearts to God. And whatever you do, in word or deed, do everything in the name of the Lord Jesus, giving thanks to God the Father through him. (Colossians 3:12–17)

May the Spirit guide you on your adventure of life. St. Paul, pray for us!

Where Paul Went

Let's say that you live in Southern California. You're sitting out on the beach one day, just you and a couple of your friends. All of the sudden, in a flash of light, you have a vision of God. Jesus himself appears to you and begins speaking to you. Your first inclination might be to apply heavier sunscreen or drink more water, fearing that you must be dehydrated, but the living water (see John 7:37) is standing before you, assuring you of his divine presence. He assures you of your goodness, his unconditional love for you, and the eternal presence of his limitless mercy. He also tells you to stop sinning, for every time you sin against another, friend or foe, you sin against him, your Savior.

Then he vanishes as quickly as he arrived, and you make a promise. This won't be a pact or covenant like the others you've made and broken—you know, the kind that begin with the phrase, "Lord, if you get me out of this, I promise I will..." No, this is a promise you actually intend to keep. You are so moved by the beauty of Jesus's message that you want to share this good news of his salvation and mercy with everyone you meet.

You immediately head home to pack up a couple outfits, an iPod, your Bible (you might need that), rosary, toothbrush, and ATM card. You kiss your parents good-bye, shake a few hands, and log off your Facebook account—for good. It's time to evangelize the world, because *evangelize* means to "share the Gospel," and the Gospel is the good news that Christ just made clear to you on that beach. Is your next stop the airport or the bus station? Nice idea, but no. That's right, you don't own a car and you can't afford a plane ticket. Nope, it looks like you're going to have to make your way from San Diego to New York on foot. You can go part of the way on horseback and by boat—if you're lucky. (Of course, a boat won't help you get over the mountains in your path.) You'll be stopping at several cities along the way; cities where people not only want nothing to do with you, but where you'll be threatened with death (and almost killed) for sharing the things you try to share with them about God's love and personal sins.

What's the total distance of your trip? It's over 2,400 miles.

Would you still go?

Paul did.

He didn't evangelize because he wanted to make a name for himself. He already had a reputation, and it wasn't a good one with the people he was now supposed to call family. Paul wasn't in it for the popularity, the power, the title, or the money. Paul went out and risked his life every day because the news he had received was *just that good*. He believed in it so deeply that he stopped at nothing to preach it to the ends of the earth. What news was he spreading, and what truth was he preaching? The truth contained in the Gospels, printed in *your Bible,* sitting on *your nightstand* or *your coffee table.* The same words we utter out of habit, read out of fear, study filled with confusion, or recite with boredom are the words that kept Paul's feet moving for thousands of miles around the ancient Mediterranean world.

According to the Acts of the Apostles, St. Paul's passport would have been stamped on just about every page. Here's a rundown of where Paul went, approximately in order:

45–48	Paul's first journey (Galatia)
50–52	Paul's second journey (Greece)
53–58	Paul's third journey (Ephesus)
58	Paul in Jerusalem
58–60	Paul in Caesarea
60–61	Paul's fourth journey (Rome)
61–63	Paul's first Roman captivity
67	Paul's second captivity
67	Paul is executed

WHAT PAUL WROTE

St. Paul was threatened by the elements, peers, imprisonment, death, and the evil one himself, yet he kept moving, and he kept writing.

On the pages that follow, we have provided introductory information for personal and group Scripture study. While it is impossible to do justice to the inspired word of God in just a couple of pages, these overviews—if prayerfully read and examined—offer insights that may be profitable before, during, and after you read St. Paul's writings. Each overview will give you some central themes of the epistle, as well as some specific verses that are emblematic of the various points that St. Paul was making to his audiences.

You might want to use the summaries as an introduction for private study. You can also use them in a group study as you begin to discuss the various overarching themes of each work. The point is this: Use them. St. Paul's writings are a beautiful gift from God and are meant to be explored. Prayerfully read through these sections in conjunction with the letters of St. Paul themselves, and watch how the second reading at Sunday Mass—and, most importantly, your soul—comes to life.

Romans

The letter of St. Paul to the Romans is a very special epistle. It displays the apostle's theological brilliance as well as his deep love and spirituality. It is St. Paul's longest and most influential letter.

St. Paul wrote the letter to introduce himself to the Christians who lived in the heavily populated city of Rome and also to prepare them for his upcoming visit. The apostle had heard reports of trouble amidst the various Christian converts in the area. Through the ministry of the apostles, many people—both Jews and Gentiles—came to faith in Christ. The converts changed their lives and fell madly in love with our Savior.

Unfortunately, however, problems arose. Some of the Jewish converts to Christianity believed that Jewish ceremonies like circumcision were still required before one could be a full member of the Church. Thus, some of the Jewish Christians were trying to force the Gentile Christians to get circumcised in addition to being baptized. This provoked great controversy. Some thought that circumcision was still necessary, while others thought that baptism was enough.

St. Paul's letter to the Romans was his authoritative answer to this issue: *Only baptism is required to be a Christian; circumcision is a sign of the Old Covenant, and it is unable to give the saving grace that baptism gives.* Circumcision is not a sacrament. It is not required to be a follower of Christ. Baptism, as a sacrament of faith, is sufficient.

Because this letter is so intricate and complicated, don't be discouraged if you find it confusing at places. St. Paul deals with many complex issues and themes. Here are some of the key themes and verses you'll discover in this letter:

The power of the Gospel: "For I am not ashamed of the Gospel: it is the power of God for salvation to every one who has faith." (Romans 1:16)

The universal effect of sin: "All have sinned and fall short of the glory of God." (Romans 3:23)

Faith, grace, and salvation: "Therefore, since we are justified by faith, we have peace with God through our Lord Jesus Christ. Through him we have obtained access to this grace in which we stand, and we rejoice in our hope of sharing the glory of God. More than that, we rejoice in our sufferings, knowing that suffering produces endurance, and endurance produces character, and character produces hope, and hope does not disappoint us, because God's love has been poured into our hearts through the Holy Spirit which has been given to us." (Romans 5:1–5)

Life through Christ: "So you also must consider yourselves dead to sin and alive to God in Christ Jesus." (Romans 6:11)

The power of baptism: "Do you not know that all of us who have been baptized into Christ Jesus were baptized into his death? We were buried therefore with him by Baptism into death, so that as Christ was raised from the dead by the glory of the Father, we too might walk in newness of life." (Romans 6:3–4)

ST. PAUL,

IT IS SO SCARY TO
HAVE A SHAKING UP
OF OUR ENTIRE WORLD-
VIEW AND ALL OUR
BELIEFS. WE FEEL
WE HAVE NO SOLID
GROUND AND WONDER
IF WE'VE DONE ANY-
THING RIGHT. AND
WHAT TO DO NOW.
HELP US TO KNOW
THAT CHANGING BE-
LIEFS CAN BE FOR
THE BETTER. EVEN
WHEN SCARY. AND
WE WILL FEEL SOL-
ID AGAIN. AMEN.

We are children of God: "For all who are led by the Spirit of God are sons of God. For you did not receive the spirit of slavery to fall back into fear, but you have received the spirit of sonship. When we cry, 'Abba! Father!' it is the Spirit himself bearing witness with our spirit that we are children of God. and if children, then heirs, heirs of God and fellow heirs with Christ, provided we suffer with him in order that we may also be glorified with him." (Romans 8:14–17)

God's sovereign purpose: "We know that in everything God works for good with those who love him, who are called according to his purpose." (Romans 8:28)

Christian transformation: "Do not be conformed to this world but be transformed by the renewal of your mind, that you may prove what is the will of God, what is good and acceptable and perfect." (Romans 12:2)

First and Second Corinthians

The city of Corinth was a busy place. A lot of trading was done in the city, and it was known for its great economic prosperity and success. Attracting many people from all walks of life, Corinth was also known for its rampant sinfulness. It was kind of like the Las Vegas of its time.

St. Paul himself had helped to start the Church in Corinth, but he was unable to remain in the city and oversee its spiritual growth (see Acts 18:1–18). Unfortunately, a lot of scandalous behavior began to emerge within the Church in Corinth after the apostle left. Through word of mouth, St. Paul heard about some of the gross sins the Christians had been committing, and he wrote to encourage them to reject their immoral behavior and to renew their commitment to a life grounded in the love of Christ (see 1 Corinthians 10:6–13).

First and Second Corinthians are very powerful letters, and they address a lot of the struggles we face in the Christian life. Peer pressure isn't something new. It is something that Christians living in the early Church had to face as well. And in these letters St. Paul is very understanding and sensitive to human weakness yet clear about how we should respond to struggles in the Christian life. Like a good father, St. Paul is lovingly firm in his guidance (see 2 Corinthians 10–13).

He reminds us that everything we have—even our bodies—belongs to Christ (see 1 Corinthians 6:12–20), and tells us we should pursue love above all things (see 1 Corinthians 12–14).

The Christian life is not easy, but Christ's love and grace are sufficient to get us through the difficult times and overcome our weaknesses (see 2 Corinthians 8–10). Here are some of the key themes and verses we can discover in these letters:

Christian unity and maturity are very important: "I appeal to you, brethren, by the name of our Lord Jesus Christ, that all of you agree and that there be no dissensions among you, but that you be united in the same mind and the same judgment." (1 Corinthians 1:10).

Marriage and celibacy are both sacred callings, and they should be treasured: "I wish that all were as I myself am. But each has his own special gift from God, one of one kind and one of another." (1 Corinthians 7:7)

The Eucharist is sacred and must be treated with great reverence: "Whoever, therefore, eats the bread or drinks the cup of the Lord in an unworthy manner will be guilty of profaning the body and blood of the Lord. Let a man examine himself, and so eat of the bread and drink of the cup. For any one who eats and drinks without discerning the body eats and drinks judgment upon himself." (1 Corinthians 11:27–29)

Love is the greatest of all spiritual gifts: "So faith, hope, love abide, these three; but the greatest of these is love." (1 Corinthians 13:13)

Christ will comfort us in our suffering: "For as we share abundantly in Christ's sufferings, so through Christ we share abundantly in comfort too." (2 Corinthians 1:5).

Christ has transformed us by the power of his love: "Therefore, if any one is in Christ, he is a new creation; the old has passed away, behold the new has come." (2 Corinthians 5:17)

Be generous to God and those around you: "He who sows sparingly will also reap sparingly, and he who sows bountifully will also reap bountifully." (2 Corinthians 9:6)

God can overcome every human weakness: "'My grace is sufficient for you, for my power is made perfect in weakness.' I will all the more gladly boast in my weaknesses, that the power of Christ may rest upon me...for when I am weak, then I am strong." (2 Corinthians 12:9–10)

Galatians

Although not quite as long (or as complicated) as his epistle to the Romans, the letter of St. Paul to the Galatians is also focused on this primary question: *Does one have to be circumcised in order to be a full Christian?* Again, as he said in Romans, the answer is *no*. Circumcision is not necessary. It does not communicate grace. Baptism—not circumcision—communicates grace and gives us entrance into God's covenant family.

St. Paul wrote to persuade Christians that the ceremonial laws and practices of the old covenant are no longer necessary. In fact, they are now harmful. Through the person and work of Jesus Christ, the Old Covenant ceremonies (works of the law like circumcision, diet restrictionsm, and animal sacrifices) are retired. Jesus set us free from these ceremonial practices of the old covenant. Returning to them would be rejecting the work of Christ and would do great spiritual damage.

Before Jesus came, circumcision was the way in which someone entered God's covenant community (see Leviticus 12:3). However, the life, death and resurrection of Jesus brought about a *New Covenant* which is much more powerful and will never end. In Jesus we are set free from the Old Covenant curses (see Galatians 3:13) and have become a "new creation" in Christ (Galatians 6:15). Jesus's work fulfilled the old covenant and established the new covenant of faith (see Galatians 3:7) by way of baptism (see Galatians 3:27). This new covenant is much more personal than the old. Through Jesus Christ we have become adopted children of God (see Galatians 4:1–7).

The important thing to focus on in this letter is the centrality of Jesus in everything. Jesus is our salvation. He gave up his human life in order that we might receive his divine life. Through baptism we become God's divinely adopted sons and daughters. Christ gave us infinitely more than we could ever deserve or imagine. Prayerfully read through this epistle, stopping to thank God along the way for all of the many blessings and gifts you see the apostle identify in its pages.

Here are some of the key themes and verses we discover in this letter:

Faith in Christ is the key to salvation: "Man is not justified by works of the law [such as circumcision] but through faith in Jesus Christ." (Galatians 2:16)

Baptism unites us to Christ: "In Christ Jesus you are all sons of God, through faith. For as many of you as were baptized into Christ have put on Christ." (Galatians 3:26–27)

Jesus was sent into the world to make us divinely adopted sons and daughters: "God sent forth his Son, born of woman, born under the law, to redeem those who were under the law, so that we might receive adoption as sons. And because you are sons, God has sent the Spirit of his Son into our hearts, crying, 'Abba! Father!' So through God you are no longer a slave but a son, and if a son then an heir." (Galatians 4:4–7)

Faith and love are the key to the Christian life: "For in Christ Jesus neither circumcision nor uncircumcision is of any avail, but faith working through love." (Galatians 5:6)

Jesus made us free in order to love: "For you were called to freedom, brethren; only do not use your freedom as an opportunity for the flesh, but through love be servants of one another." (Galatians 5:13).

The Holy Spirit produces nine fruits: "The fruit of the Spirit is love, joy, peace, patience, kindness, goodness, faithfulness, gentleness, self-control." (Galatians 5:22–23)

We are called to live and walk in the Spirit: "If we live by the Spirit, let us also walk by the Spirit. Let us have no self-conceit, no provoking of one another, no envy of one another." (Galatians 5:25–26)

Care for others: "Bear one another's burdens, and so fulfill the law of Christ." (Galatians 6:2)

Don't lose hope when things grow difficult: "Let us not grow weary in well doing, for in due season we shall reap, if we do not lose heart. So then, as we have opportunity, let us do good to all

men, and especially to those who are of the household of faith."
(Galatians 6:9–10)

Ephesians

The mystery of Jesus Christ is both the key to our salvation and the
central theme in St. Paul's letter to the Ephesians (see Ephesians
1:9; 3:4, 9). The mystery of Christ has various dimensions. Jesus
is the Savior of the world, and he came to die on the cross for the
sins of all people—no matter what their background or former
way of life. After his death and resurrection, Jesus ascended into
heaven where he is highly exalted and is seated at the right hand
of the Father (see Ephesians 1:20–23).

St. Paul spent a lot of time going through these things because he
believed that they were vitally important. Although they occurred
in the past, Christ's life, death, and resurrection continue to have
power and relevance in the modern period. Even though Jesus
isn't currently walking the earth in bodily form, his presence is still
real and powerful through the life and ministry of the Church—
in fact, the two are joined together according to Ephesians 5:32).
The Church isn't optional. It is a necessary part of Christ's lasting
gift to his people. Christ is the head and center of the Church, and
it is Christ who unites the Church (see Ephesians 5:23).

This letter is St. Paul's attempt to help his readers more fully
understand the profound graces they have received from God in
and through Jesus and his Church. As you read this, meditate on
the blessings you have received through the sacraments, and look
for guidance from the apostle about how to live out your adoptive sonship.

Here are some of the key themes and verses to discover in this letter:

God chose us to be his children before the world was created: "He chose us in him before the foundation of the world, that we should be holy and blameless before him. He destined us in love to be his sons through Jesus Christ according to the purpose of his will, to the praise of his glorious grace which he freely bestowed on us in the Beloved." (see Ephesians 1:4–6)

God's mysterious plan was to bring us home to him: "He has made known to us in all wisdom and insight the mystery of his will, according to his purpose which he set forth in Christ as a plan for the fulness of time, to unite all things in him, things in heaven and things on earth." (Ephesians 1:9–10)

God's love and mercy are the reasons for our salvation: "God, who is rich in mercy, out of the great love with which he loved us, even when we were dead through our trespasses, made us alive together with Christ (by grace you have been saved), and raised us up with him, and made us sit with him in the heavenly places in Christ Jesus." (Ephesians 2:4–6)

Salvation is by grace through faith: "For by grace you have been saved through faith; and this is not your own doing, it is the gift of God—not because of works, lest any man should boast." (Ephesians 2:8–9)

We are called to unity in the Spirit: "There is one body and one Spirit, just as you were called to the one hope that belongs to your call, one Lord, one faith, one baptism, one God and Father of us all, who is above all and through all and in all." (Ephesians 4:4–6)

We are to imitate Christ: "Be imitators of God, as beloved children. And walk in love, as Christ loved us and gave himself up for us, a fragrant offering and sacrifice to God." (Ephesians 5:1–2)

We need the truth and love of Christ to win the battle for our souls: "Take the whole armor of God, that you may be able to withstand in the evil day, and having done all, to stand." (Ephesians 6:13)

Philippians

The letter of St. Paul to the Philippians is an epistle of encouragement and thanksgiving. The Church in Philippi was always eager to support the work of Christ no matter what the cost, and the apostle wanted to express his profound gratitude for their prayers and assistance. This is a very personal letter from the pen of St. Paul. Unlike his letters to the Romans and the Galatians, there were no big debates or controversies to be resolved. Thus, Philippians is also rather informal in style—in a way similar to how we could write close friends.

The apostle encourages his readers to follow his example of imitating Jesus in all things, but especially in terms of his *servanthood* (see Philippians 2:1–11; 2:12–18). St. Paul was committed to his Savior in all and through all. The Christian life is not easy, but the apostle Paul was adamant about the fact that the joy of knowing Christ is worth every struggle.

As you read through this short epistle, look for ways you can imitate St. Paul's servanthood and more fully receive the joy of knowing Jesus in your own life. Here are some of the key themes and verses you'll discover in this letter:

Love Jesus in all things: "With full courage now as always Christ will be honored in my body, whether by life or by death. For to me to live is Christ, and to die is gain." (Philippians 1:20–21)

Suffering is a part of the Christian life: "It has been granted to you that for the sake of Christ you should not only believe in him but also suffer for his sake." (Philippians 1:29)

Christ was the supreme servant: "[Though Jesus] was in the form of God, [he] did not count equality with God a thing to be grasped, but emptied himself, taking the form of a servant, being born in the likeness of men.... He humbled himself and became obedient unto death.... Therefore God has highly exalted him." (Philippians 2:5–11)

Nothing compares to the joy found in knowing Christ Jesus: "But whatever gain I had, I counted as loss for the sake of Christ. Indeed I count everything as loss because of the surpassing worth of knowing Christ Jesus my Lord. For his sake I have suffered the loss of all things, and count them as refuse, in order that I might gain Christ." (Philippians 3:7–8)

Our real home is in heaven with Jesus: "Our commonwealth is in heaven, and from it we await a Savior, the Lord Jesus Christ, who will change our lowly body to be like his glorious body." (Philippians 3:20–21)

Only in Jesus will we find eternal joy and happiness: "Rejoice in the Lord always; again I will say, Rejoice.... The peace of God, which passes all understanding will keep your hearts and your minds in Christ Jesus." (Philippians 4:4–7)

As Christians, think about these things: "Finally, brethren, whatever is true, whatever is honorable, whatever is just, whatever is pure, whatever is lovely, whatever is gracious, if there is any excellence, if there is anything worthy of praise, think about these things." (Philippians 4:8)

Colossians

The letter of St. Paul to the Colossians is an interesting epistle. Unlike some of the others, St. Paul did not personally found or even visit the Church in Colossae (see Colossians 2:1). St. Paul had heard about the Colossian Church through a man named Epaphras (see Colossians 1:7; 4:12) who informed the apostle about the struggles of this young Christian community.

Apparently some rabble-rousers were attempting to persuade people that the faith of the Gentile Christians was inadequate. The Jews of the time were very critical of the Gentile converts because they were uncircumcised. Again, St. Paul reiterates the fact that circumcision is a sign of the Old Covenant, and it is no longer necessary because of Christ's death and resurrection. He is very pastoral in his tone and reassures the Gentile Christians that they are full-fledged members of God's covenantal family by way of faith and baptism (see Colossians 1:21–23; 2:11–12).

St. Paul stresses the fact Jesus Christ is at the center of reality and should be at the center of our lives. Christ reigns supreme. He is almighty and over all. God is sovereign. Nothing escapes his influence, authority, and power. And while there is opposition to Christ and his Church, the battle is as good as won. Christ has triumphed over all opposing forces (see Colossians 2:15–23).

Because he is supreme, Christ is sufficient for our every need. Through baptism we are united to Christ (see Colossians 2:12), and in Christ we encounter the fullness of life, love, and salvation. Hence, we should strive to conform our lives to the saving Gospel of Jesus Christ. We must be vigilant in our prayer and commitment to the grace of Christ, for in it we find our strength and power (see Colossians 4:2).

As you read this epistle, meditate on the various passages which refer to the supremacy of Jesus and think of ways you can give glory to him through your words and actions. Here are some of the key themes and verses in this letter:

Christ is central and supreme: "[Christ] is the image of the invisible God, the first-born of all creation; for in him all things were created." (Colossians 1:15–16)

Our suffering unites us to Christ and aids the Church: "I rejoice in my sufferings for your sake, and in my flesh I complete what is lacking in Christ's afflictions for the sake of his body, that is, the church." (Colossians 1:24)

We must be heavenly minded: "Set your minds on things that are above, not on things that are on earth.... Your life is hid with Christ in God." (Colossians 3:2–3)

Love must be central: "Above all these put on love, which binds everything together in perfect harmony." (Colossians 3:14)

Whatever we do should be done for the glory of God: "Whatever your task, work heartily, as serving the Lord and not men, knowing that from the Lord you will receive the inheritance as your reward; you are serving the Lord Christ." (Colossians 3:23–24)

First and Second Thessalonians

The letters of St. Paul to the Thessalonians are very pastoral. The apostle wrote to a group of recent converts who were experiencing great persecution. He offered his prayers, thoughts, and paternal encouragement in their time of great trial and difficulty. He commended them for their growth in faith, hope, and love (see 1 Thessalonians 1:3; 3:6; 5:8), offered no big criticisms or reprimands, and urged them to remain steady in the Christian journey (see 1 Thessalonians 4:1; 5:11).

As in all his epistles, the apostle urged his readers to be vigilant in love (see 1 Thessalonians 3:12) and holiness (see 1 Thessalonians 3:13; 5:23). He reminded them that Jesus will one day return in glory to save us from wrath and give us salvation (see 1 Thessalonians 1:10; 5:9; 2 Thessalonians 1:10). No one knows when Jesus will return, and that is why we must remain steadfast at all times, ready for his arrival (see 1 Thessalonians 5:1–11). He offers great hope to his readers, assuring them that those in Christ will be escorted to the glory of heaven just like Jesus himself had been carried to heaven (see 1 Thessalonians 4:14–18).

Here are some of the key themes and verses in these letters:

God chooses his people: "For we know, brethren beloved by God, that he has chosen you." (1 Thessalonians 1:4; see also 2 Thessalonians 2:13)

Pursue holiness and flee immorality: "For this is the will of God, your sanctification: that you abstain from immorality; that each one of you knows how to control his own body in holiness and honor." (1 Thessalonians 4:3–4)

All who die in the love of Christ will rise again in glory: "For since we believe that Jesus died and rose again, even so, through Jesus, God will bring with him those who have fallen asleep... the dead in Christ will rise." (1 Thessalonians 4:14–16; see also 2 Thessalonians 1:10–12)

Until Christ returns, be vigilant in faith, hope and love: "Let us be sober, and put on the breastplate of faith and love, and for a helmet the hope of salvation." (1 Thessalonians 5:8)

Do not depart from the teachings and guidance of the Church: "Stand firm and hold to the traditions which you were taught by us, either by word of mouth or by letter." (2 Thessalonians 2:15)

First and Second Timothy

The letters of St. Paul to Timothy are unique among the apostle's writings. Timothy was stationed in the Church at Ephesus in order to help it recover from the damage of some false teachers who had been deceiving God's people (1 Timothy 1:3–7; 6:3–5).

In a very loving way, the apostle encourages Timothy to remain firm in the truth (see 1 Timothy 4:6–7; 6:20). Sound doctrine is important; St. Paul is adamant about the fact that God's people must be taught nothing less than the fullness of truth (see 2 Timothy 1:13–14; 4:2–3). As a spiritual mentor, St. Paul encourages Timothy to continue preaching the Gospel message of Jesus Christ long after the apostle has passed on to the next life (see 2 Timothy 4:6–8). Following Christ is not an easy task, but the apostle urges Timothy to take courage and strength from his example of faithfulness (see 2 Timothy 3:10–14).

St. Paul instructs his young friend to "guard" the truth of the Gospel (see 2 Timothy 1:14). The truth of God is sacred. It is not to be modified or adjusted to fit the trivial preferences of mere humans (see 2 Timothy 4:3–5).

Here are some of the key themes and verses we discover in these letters:

There is one God and Mediator: "There is one God, and there is one mediator between God and men, the man Christ Jesus, who gave himself as a ransom for all." (1 Timothy 2:5–6)

The Church is a pillar of truth: "The church of the living God [is] the pillar and bulwark of the truth." (1 Timothy 3:15)

God doesn't make junk: "For everything created by God is good, and nothing is to be rejected if it is received with thanksgiving." (1 Timothy 4:4)

Christians should care for one another: "If any one does not provide for his relatives, and especially for his own family, he has disowned the faith and is worse than an unbeliever." (1 Timothy 5:8)

Fight for the truth and holiness: "Aim at righteousness, godliness, faith, love, steadfastness, gentleness. Fight the good fight of the faith." (1 Timothy 6:11–12)

Have confidence in Christ: "I am not ashamed, for I know whom I have believed, and I am sure that he is able to guard until that Day what has been entrusted to me." (2 Timothy 1:12)

Scripture is sacred and inspired by God himself: "All scripture is inspired by God and profitable for teaching, for reproof, for correction, and for training in righteousness, that the man of God may be complete, equipped for every good work." (2 Timothy 3:16–17)

Titus

Titus and St. Paul had worked together to evangelize parts of the Island of Crete. When the apostle left Crete to go spread the saving message of Jesus to other places, Titus remained to organize the Christian converts and help them form a solid community.

As with his letters to Timothy, St. Paul is very pastoral in his advice and counsel to Titus. He exhorts him to remain firm in the unwavering truth of Christ (see Titus 1:10–16; 2:1). The apostle also spends time giving Titus advice about how discern which men are worthy to be ordained to the priesthood (see Titus 1:5). Because the call to priesthood (that is, to be an "elder") is a sacred vocation, this discernment should be done very carefully. St. Paul instructs Titus to evaluate a candidate's character and family when considering someone for ordination (see Titus 1:7–8). The reason for this is simple: People will learn about Christ through the life-style and actions of Christian leaders. Spirit-led discernment and wisdom are essential.

While this is especially true for priests and bishops, it is true for all Christians. St. Paul reminds Titus that all believers should be faithful and holy in word and action (see Titus 2:7; 3:1–14). We are called to be Christ to all people whether they are fellow Christians or not (see Titus 2:2–10; 3:1–2).

Here are some of the key themes and verses you'll discover in this letter:

We can have great confidence in the saving promises of God: "Paul, a servant of God and an apostle of Jesus Christ, to further the faith of God's elect and their knowledge of the truth which accords with godliness, in hope of eternal life which God, who never lies, promised ages ago." (Titus 1:1–2)

Pursue holiness in all things: "Show yourself in all respects a model of good deeds, and in your teaching show integrity, gravity, and sound speech." (Titus 2:7–8)

Avoid mean-spirited interactions: "Speak evil of no one…avoid quarreling." (Titus 3:2)

The grace of Christ is the key to salvation: "[God] saved us, not because of deeds done by us in righteousness, but in virtue of his own mercy, by the washing of regeneration and renewal in the Holy Spirit, which he poured out upon us richly through Jesus Christ our Savior, so that we might be justified by his grace and become heirs in hope of eternal life." (Titus 2:5–7)

Philemon

The letter of St. Paul to Philemon is the shortest epistle from the pen of St. Paul. This is a moving letter that gives a very intimate glimpse into the apostle's heart. It is written to a slave owner named Philemon, a woman named Apphia (possibly Philemon's wife), and a man named Archippus (possibly Philemon's son). St. Paul wrote this letter requesting that Philemon welcome back one of his runaway slaves (a man named Onesimus).

Apparently, Onesimus had originally been "useless" and unfaithful to his master, perhaps even stealing from Philemon (see Philemon 1:11, 18). However, God's grace is powerful and it seems that Onesimus had a conversion to Christ through the ministry of St. Paul. The apostle sent Onesimus back to his master (see Philemon 1:12) and wrote to Philemon encouraging him to embrace Onesimus as a brother in Christ (see Philemon 1:16).

This epistle, though short, is a beautiful glimpse into true Christian conversion, love, mercy, and forgiveness. As you read it, meditate on the power of God's loving mercy and forgiveness to transform every part of our life and being.

Thematic Concordance of Paul's Writings

Do you want to see for yourself what the Holy Spirit through St. Paul had to share about the following topics? Take the time to read and pray through them on your own.

ANGER
Ephesians 4:26
Ephesians 4:31
Colossians 3:8
Colossians 3:19
1 Timothy 2:8

CHASTITY/SEXUALITY
Romans 6:12–13
Romans 12:1
Romans 13:13
1 Corinthians 6:9
1 Corinthians 6:15
2 Corinthians 12:21
Galatians 5:19
Ephesians 4:19
1 Thessalonians 4:5

CHURCH/COMMUNITY
Romans 12:4–5
1 Corinthians 10:17
1 Corinthians 12:12–13
1 Corinthians 12:20
Ephesians 4:3–4
Colossians 3:15
Philippians 1:27

DATING
2 Corinthians 6:14
2 Corinthians 7:1
Galatians 5:23
1 Thessalonians 4:3–4
1 Thessalonians 4:7
1 Timothy 2:9
2 Timothy 1:7

DEATH
Romans 5:10, 12, 14, 17, 21
Romans 6:3–4, 9–10, 23
Romans 8:2, 6
1 Corinthians 15:21, 54–55
2 Corinthians 1:9–10
2 Corinthians 4:12
2 Corinthians 7:10
Philippians 1:21
Philippians 2:8
Philippians 3:10
Colossians 3:5

DISCIPLESHIP
Romans 4:16
2 Corinthians 7:1
Galatians 2:20

Galatians 5:25
Galatians 6:16
Ephesians 4:24
1 Thessalonians 3:13
1 Thessalonians 4:3–4, 7
2 Timothy 1:9

DOUBT
Romans 4:20
Romans 6:8
Galatians 3:22
Ephesians 1:19
Philippians 1:29
1 Thessalonians 4:14
1 Timothy 1:16

ETERNAL LIFE
Romans 2:7
Romans 5:21
Romans 6:23
Galatians 6:8
Philippians 3:20
Colossians 1:5, 16, 20
1 Timothy 1:2
1 Timothy 6:12

EUCHARIST
1 Corinthians 10:16–17
1 Corinthians 11:23, 26–28
Ephesians 2:13
Ephesians 5:30
Colossians 1:20

EVANGELIZATION
1 Corinthians 9:12, 23
2 Corinthians 1:7
Philippians 2:17–18
1 Thessalonians 2:8
1 Timothy 6:18
2 Timothy 1:8
2 Timothy 2:3

DRINKING/PARTYING
Romans 2:19
Romans 13:12–13
1 Corinthians 4:5
1 Corinthians 15:34
1 Thessalonians 5:8
Galatians 5:21
Ephesians 5:8,11
Ephesians 6:12

FAITH
Romans 1:12, 17
Romans 3:28,31
Romans 4:16,20
Romans 5:2
Romans 10:17
Romans 12:6
1 Corinthians 2:5
1 Corinthians 13:13
1 Corinthians 15:14, 17
2 Corinthians 5:7
Galatians 2:20
Galatians 3:23

Galatians 5:5
Ephesians 2:8
Ephesians 3:12, 17
Ephesians 6:16
Colossians 1:4
1 Thessalonians 3:7, 10
2 Thessalonians 1:3–4
1 Timothy 1:5
1 Timothy 4:12
1 Timothy 6:12
2 Timothy 4:7

FAMILY
Romans 8:14, 16–17, 19, 21
Galatians 3:26
Galatians 4:6
Galatians 6:10
Ephesians 3:15
Ephesians 5:1
Ephesians 6:1, 4
Philippians 2:15
1 Thessalonians 2:11
1 Thessalonians 5:5
I Timothy 3:4
1 Timothy 5:4, 8

FEAR
Romans 8:15
2 Corinthians 5:6–8
Ephesians 6:20
Philippians 1:20
1 Thessalonians 2:2

FUTURE/VOCATION
Romans 8:28, 38
Romans 9:21
Ephesians 1:11
Ephesians 2:10
Philippians 2:13
2 Thessalonians 1:11
1 Timothy 6:19

GOD THE FATHER
Romans 8:15
1 Corinthians 8:6
Galatians 4:6
Ephesians 2:18
Ephesians 3:14
Ephesians 5:20
Philippians 2:11
Colossians 3:17

GRACE
Romans 1:5
Romans 3:24
Romans 5:2, 20–21
Romans 6:1, 14–15
Romans 11:6
1 Corinthians 15:10
2 Corinthians 6:1
2 Corinthians 9:8, 14
2 Corinthians 12:9
Galatians 2:21
Ephesians 4:7, 29
Philippians 4:23

GREED/MATERIALISM
Romans 1:29
Romans 7:7
Ephesians 5:3
Colossians 3:5
1 Timothy 3:3
1 Timothy 6:10

HOLY SPIRIT
Romans 5:5
Romans 5:2, 4–5
Romans 8:24–25
Romans 14:17
Romans 15:16
1 Corinthians 6:19
1 Corinthians 12:3
1 Corinthians 13:13
2 Corinthians 1:7, 10
2 Corinthians 3:12
2 Corinthians 13:13
Ephesians 1:13
Ephesians 4:4
Philippians 3:12
Colossians 1:5, 23, 27
1 Thessalonians 1:5–6
1 Thessalonians 4:8
1 Timothy 4:10
2 Timothy 1:14
Titus 1:2

JUDGMENT
Romans 2:1–2

Romans 5:12
Romans 14:3–4, 10
1 Corinthians 2:15
1 Corinthians 4:3, 5
1 Corinthians 6:2
2 Thessalonians 1:5
1 Timothy 5:24
2 Timothy 4:1
2 Timothy 4:8

LOVE
Romans 5:5, 8
Romans 8:35, 39
Romans 12:9–10
Romans 13:8, 10
1 Corinthians 2:9
1 Corinthians 13:1–13
2 Corinthians 5:14
2 Corinthians 13:13
Galatians 5:6
Galatians 5:22
Ephesians 2:4
Ephesians 5:2
Philippians 1:9
Colossians 3:14
1 Thessalonians 5:8
1 Timothy 4:12
2 Timothy 1:7

MARRIAGE
1 Corinthians 7:3–4, 10–13
1 Corinthians 7:14, 16

1 Corinthians 11:2–3
Ephesians 5:23–25, 28, 33
Colossians 3:18–19
1 Thessalonians 4:4

PRAYER
Romans 8:26
Romans 12:12
1 Corinthians 7:5
1 Corinthians 14:14–15
Ephesians 6:18
Philippians 1:9
Philippians 4:6
Colossians 4:2
1 Thessalonians 5:17
1 Timothy 2:8
1 Timothy 4:5

PRIESTHOOD/ AUTHORITY
Romans 1:5
1 Corinthians 7:35
1 Corinthians 9:23
1 Corinthians 15:5
2 Corinthians 4:11
2 Corinthians 12:10
Galatians 1:18
Philippians 1:29
Philippians 2:30
1 Timothy 3:1–2
1 Timothy 5:17
Titus 1:7

SALVATION
Romans 1:16
Romans 5:9–10
Romans 8:24
Romans 13:11
1 Corinthians 3:15
2 Corinthians 6:2
Ephesians 1:13
Philippians 2:12
1 Thessalonians 5:8–9
1 Timothy 2:4
2 Timothy 3:15

SIN
Romans 5:12–14
Romans 6:11–12, 14, 22–23
Romans 7:17, 20
Romans 8:10
1 Corinthians 6:18
1 Corinthians 8:13
1 Corinthians 15:56
2 Corinthians 5:21

TEMPTATION
Romans 7:19, 21
1 Corinthians 7:5
1 Corinthians 10:6, 13
1 Corinthians 14:20
Galatians 6:1
Ephesians 6:12–13
Colossians 3:5
1 Thessalonians 3:3

Cameron, Fr. Peter John (ed). Praying with Saint Paul: Daily Reflections on the Letters of the Apostle Paul (San Francisco: Ignatius, 2008).

Hahn, Scott. *A Father Who Keeps His Promises: God's Covenant Love in Scripture* (Ann Arbor, Mich.: Servant, 1998).

————. *Answering Common Objections* (CD set 1, St. Joseph Communications).

————. *Romanism in Romans: A Bible Study of the Book of Romans* (CD set, St. Joseph Communications).

————. *Salvation History* (CD set, St. Joseph Communications).

————. *The Mystery: A Bible Study of the Book of Ephesians* (CD set, St. Joseph Communications).

————. *Understanding The Scriptures: A Complete Course on Bible Study* (Chicago: Midwest Theological Forum, 2005).

Ignatius Catholic Study Bible: The Acts of the Apostles, with Curtis Mitch (San Francisco: Ignatius, 2002).

Ignatius Catholic Study Bible: The First and Second Letters of Saint Paul to the Corinthians, with Curtis Mitch (San Francisco: Ignatius, 2004).

Ignatius Catholic Study Bible: The Letters of St. Paul to the Galatians and Ephesians, with Curtis Mitch (San Francisco: Ignatius, 2005).

Ignatius Catholic Study Bible: The Letters of St. Paul to the Philippians, Colossians, and Philemon, with Curtis Mitch (San Francisco: Ignatius, 2005).

Ignatius Catholic Study Bible: The Letter of Saint Paul to the Romans, with Curtis Mitch (San Francisco: Ignatius, 2003).

Ignatius Catholic Study Bible: The Letters of St. Paul to the Thessalonians, Timothy, and Titus, with Curtis Mitch (San Francisco: Ignatius, 2005).

Pacwa, Mitch. *St. Paul: Jubilee Year of the Apostle Paul Edition: A Bible Study for Catholics* (Huntington, Ind: Our Sunday Visitor, 2008).

Pitre, Brant. *The Apostle Paul: Unlocking the Mysteries of His Theology* (CD set, Catholic Productions).

Wright, N.T. *Paul: His Fresh Perspective* (Minneapolis: Fortress Press, 2005).

———. *What Saint Paul Really Said: Was Paul of Tarsus the Real Founder of Christianity?* (Grand Rapids: Eerdmans, 1997).

Wright, N.T. *Acts for Everyone: Part One* (Louisville, Ky.: Westminster John Knox, 2007).

———. *Acts for Everyone: Part Two* (Louisville, Ky.: Westminster John Knox, 2008).

———. *Paul for Everyone: 1 Corinthians* (Louisville, Ky.: Westminster John Knox, 2004).

———. *Paul for Everyone: 2 Corinthians* (Louisville, Ky.: Westminster John Knox, 2004).

———. *Paul for Everyone: Galatians and Thessalonians* (Louisville, Ky.: Westminster John Knox, 2004).

———. *Paul for Everyone: The Pastoral Letters* (Louisville, Ky.: Westminster John Knox, 2004).

———. *Paul for Everyone: The Prison Letters* (Louisville, Ky.: Westminster John Knox, 2004).

———. *Paul for Everyone: Romans: Part One* (Louisville, Ky.: Westminster John Knox, 2004).

————. *Paul for Everyone: Romans: Part Two* (Louisville, Ky.: Westminster John Knox, 2004).

Note: N.T. "Tom" Wright is one of the most brilliant "Pauline" scholars in the world today. His research has done much to help further the understanding of St. Paul. We recommend his books even though he is not a Catholic (he is an Anglican bishop), with the understanding that the official teaching of the Catholic Church is to be followed at all times on all topics. All of the other authors are Catholic.)

1. Peter Kreeft, *Reading and Praying the New Testament* (Ann Arbor, MI:Servant, 1992), p. 50.

2. Ronald Knox, *The Hidden Stream* (San Francisco: Ignatius, 1953, 2003), p. 96.

3. Richard John Neuhaus, "The Naked Public Square: A Metaphor Reconsidered," http://www.firstthings.com/article/2008/01/the-naked-public-square-a-metaphor-reconsidered.

4. Quoted in Michael White and John Gribbin, *Stephen Hawking: A Life in Science* (Washington, D.C.: Joseph Henry Press, 2002), p. 172.

5. Council of Trent, session 6, chapter 4.

6. Keiki Hendrix, *Everyday Christian*, Christmas Classics: "The Man and the Birds" by Paul Harvey December 17, 2010, http://www.everydaychristian.com/blogs/post/christmas_classics_the_man_and_the_birds_by_paul_harvey.

7. Benedict XVI, "St Paul and the Spirit," General Audience, Saint Peter's Square, Wednesday, 15 November 2006, http://www.vatican.va/holy_father/benedict_xvi/audiences/2006/documents/hf_ben-xvi_aud_20061115_en.html.

8. St. Gregory of Nyssa, *De beatitudinibus*, 1:PG 44,1200D (quoted in *CCC* 1803).

9. Rev. Raneiro Cantalamessa, *Mary: Mirror of the Church* (Collegeville, Minn.: Liturgical, 1992), p. 17.

10. Walter Knight, Knight's Master Book of 4000 Illustrations (Grand Rapids: Eerdmans), pp. 235–236 and Hot Illustrations for Youth CD-ROM (Youth Specialties, 2001).

11. Mark Hart, *Blessed are the Bored in Spirit: A Young Catholic's Search for Meaning* (Cincinnati: Servant, 2006), p. 11.

12. Peter Kreeft, Reading and Praying the New Testament (Ann Arbor, Mich.: Servant, 1992), pp. 73–74.

13. *Dominum et Vivificantem* (The Holy Spirit in the Life of the Church and the World), section 46; emphasis in original.

14. St. Josemaría Escrivá, Furrow (London: Scepter, 1987), no. 70.

15. Deus Caritas Est, 12.

16. Quoted in Judith Fitzerald and Michael Oren Fitzgerald, *Christian Spirit* (Bloomington, Ind.: World Wisdom, 2004), p. 49.

17. Paul Lee Tan, *Encyclopedia of 7700 Illustrations* (Bible Comments, 1990).

18. Mark Hart and Todd Lemieux, *100 Things Every Catholic Teen Should Know* (Mesa, Ariz.: Life Teen, 2007), p. 259.

19. Mark Hart, *Blessed Are the Bored in Spirit*, p. 26.

20. Lee Knowles, *Catholic Book of Quotations* (Huntington, Ind.: Our Sunday Visitor, 2004), pp. 290–293.

About the Authors

Mark Hart, affectionately known to millions across the world as "The Bible Geek," serves as executive vice president for Life Teen International. An award-winning author and producer, Mark is one of the most sought-after speakers in the Catholic Church today. He is a popular guest on several radio shows and regular on Sirius/XM Satellite Radio. He is the author or coauthor of eleven books, including *Tweet Inspiration: Faith in 140 Characters (or Less)*. Hart and his family reside in Gilbert, Arizona.

Christopher Cuddy is a Catholic author and speaker.